Published by Mud House

Although every precaution has been taken in the preparation of this book, the publisher and author assume no responsibility for errors or omissions. Neither is any liability assumed for damages resulting from the use of information contained herein.

Some of the procedures and activities described in this book can be dangerous. Any person who follows these procedures and activities should do so with caution and appropriate supervision. The publisher and the author are not responsible for any accidents, injuries, damages or loss suffered by any reader of this book.

ISBN 978-1-8382889-3-8 Paper Back edition

ISBN 978-1-8382889-5-2 Hard Back edition

A special thank you goes to everyone who helped make this book, especially to the children who have road tested various ideas.

In particular I would like to thank everyone who comes to *Makers Club* at The Brewery Arts Centre in Kendal, as well as my family, who have given me their time and creativity.

Chris Barnes – March 2022

Natural Clay

Air Hardening Clay   Polymer Clay

The Clay Play Book

A book to jump start your creativity.

This book is full of information & ideas
for using Clay, Air Hardening Clay and Polymer Clay.

The projects are suitable for a wide range of age groups and abilities
from 6 - 99+ years, whether you have a kiln to fire or not.

Older children will be able to use this book on their own,
while adults can use it to initiate play with clay with younger children.

Now let's begin.

Contents

The key to the colour code used in this book is shown below

Fired Clay   Air Drying Clay   Polymer Clay

Top Tips are shown like this!

Or this!

Or this!

Introduction

This book is written to help adults and children play with clay. It shows how to make many different things with clay, air drying clay and polymer clay. You do not have to have access to a kiln to be creative with clay - in fact firing clay sets it in a way which cannot be undone without millions of years of geological processes, so firing clay ends the fun.

If you are lucky enough to have a kiln, you can turn your clay into useful and not so useful objects. If you don't fire it your clay lives on to be something new on another day. One of the beauties of real clay as a material is that it is **endlessly recyclable**.

How to use this book

Both children and their adult helpers can use this book. It is set out so that older children can use it on their own and adults can use it as a guide to help younger children. There is enough information to enable complete beginners starting from scratch to get creative with clay of all sorts. The projects in the book are designed to spark the imagination, starting points for you to launch into your own world of clay.

Projects are split into three parts:

- The first part of the book is focused on things to make with clay and air hardening clay, beginning with ways to model and join clay together. As you progress you can develop the skills for forming larger things in clay, making some of your own tools along the way.

- The second part deals with projects for polymer clay that can be baked in a normal oven to make them hard. Starting with the basics for polymer clay success, the projects combine fun ideas and simple modelling.

- The third part contains projects which can be adapted to all types of clay and also shows how the different types can be combined.

Reclaiming natural clay by soaking the dry broken pieces in a tub

Clay is a naturally occurring geological deposit which is found in abundance all over the world. It has been formed over hundreds of millions of years from the materials of the earth's crust. Primary clay is the clay which we find at the site of its formation, like the china clay found on Bodmin Moor in Cornwall. Clay is formed as granite rock decomposes over millions of years. Secondary clay is the clay which we find after it has been moved and sorted by river action and deposited in river estuaries. This clay is often more "plastic" and sticky than primary clay which makes it easier to use to make things.

Our planet has spent a very very long time making clay for us and it should be used carefully. Once fired, ceramic objects stay around for thousands of years without rotting very much at all, so do not fire things you do not need to. Reclaim your clay. It would be a shame for the archaeologists of the future to dig up the pottery we make today and wonder why we bothered to fire it - so make beautiful things!

Reclaiming your clay

When we have finished playing with natural clay it can be reclaimed and reused. To reclaim clay which is just a little dry, put it in a strong plastic bag or seal-able box with a wet sponge. It will soften up again in a day or two, depending on how dried out it was. You can then come back to it to find it revitalised, ready for kneading and re-working. This is also true of air hardening clay but may take longer if left to dry out as there is glue in this sort of clay.

To reclaim clay which is bone dry, break it into small pieces and put it in a bucket. Add just enough water to almost cover the broken clay pieces. When the clay has been *slaked*, or re-wetted, it will form a soft sludge which has to be dried enough to be *plastic*, or mould-able, again. You can do this by tipping it out onto a cloth and tying it up like a pudding bag - hanging it so that the water can drip out. Alternatively, after tipping out the excess water, just tip it out on a table top to dry over a few days. This drying sludge can be combined with stiffer plastic clay by kneading it together to make more usable clay.

Joining Clay

Because clay shrinks when it dries it sometimes cracks. Usually cracks appear along joins in your model or pot. To prevent cracking you can do these things:

- Dry the clay really slowly under a damp cloth or polythene.

- Always smudge over the joining cracks where two pieces of clay meet.

- Make the surfaces to be joined really squidgy by wetting them with slip (runny clay) and scoring the surfaces to let the moisture spread and soften the clay.

- Always try to join clay which is the same softness/hardness. Harder clay has already shrunk a bit, so it will not fit softer clay when both have fully dried.

Clay is sticky when it is soft but not at all sticky when it is dry, because of this, two pieces which stay together when soft will not always stay together after they have dried. You have to make your joined pieces of clay into one whole by blending the clay across the join .

When joining a handle to a mug use scoring and slip. It is important that the handle should be pressed on firmly and the join should be sealed with smudging.

Some Useful Tools

Here are some handy tools for clay work. They have many uses: handles of tools can be used for making dents and hollowing, The Rubber Kidney is used for slapping slabs into position, shaping clay and as a spatula. Some tools can be found in the kitchen, like miscellaneous cutlery, others can be bought from pottery suppliers - There is a list of U.K. suppliers at the end of this book.

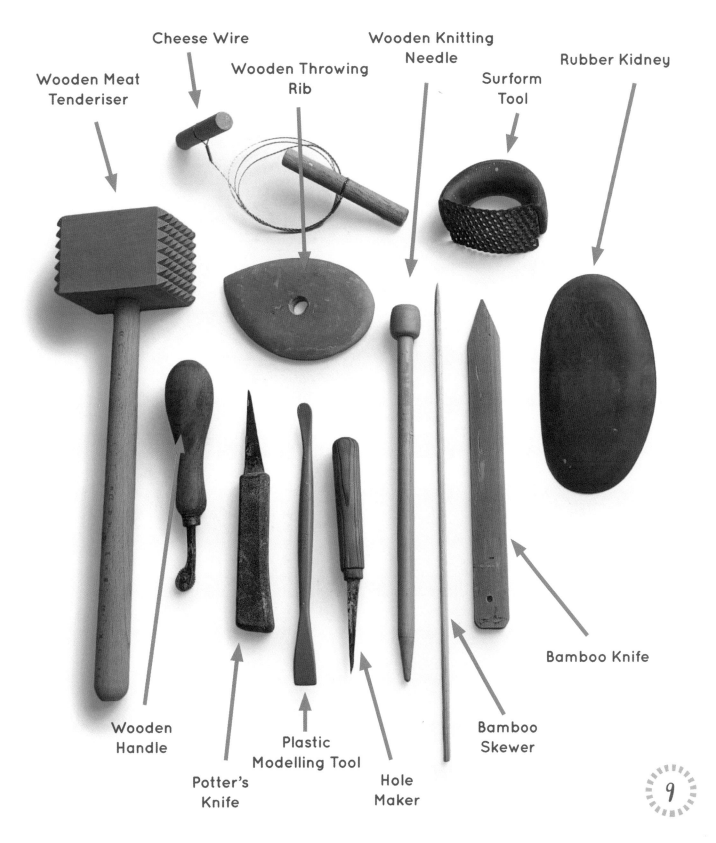

Cheese Wire

Wooden Knitting Needle

Wooden Throwing Rib

Rubber Kidney

Wooden Meat Tenderiser

Surform Tool

Wooden Handle

Plastic Modelling Tool

Potter's Knife

Hole Maker

Bamboo Skewer

Bamboo Knife

Shaping Clay

Thumb Pots

Thumb pots or pinch pots are formed by starting with a round ball of clay. Make a dent in the top with your thumb and keep squeezing the clay and turning it so that the hole you make in the ball stays in the middle.

It is a bit like inflating a clay balloon, so it is important to start with a round smooth ball of clay. Any dents and creases in the surface of the ball get stretched out and made bigger.

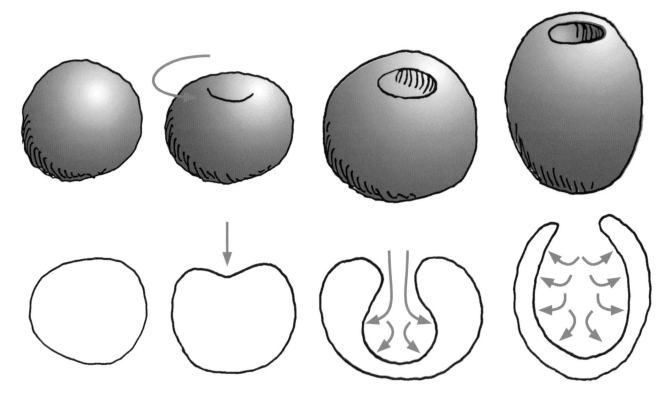

Go slowly with small pinches and squeezes to help the pot grow evenly. You will learn to gauge the thickness of the clay between your thumb and finger tips. You can make your thumb pots bigger by adding coils of clay to the rim.

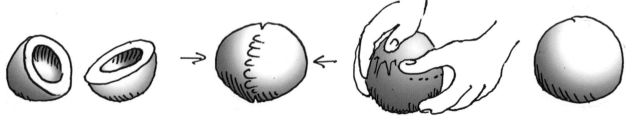

Making a hollow ball from two thumb pots joined together with slip

Building with Coils - Method 1

Ropes made of clay are often called **coils** of clay.

Make a ball of clay and flatten it for a base.

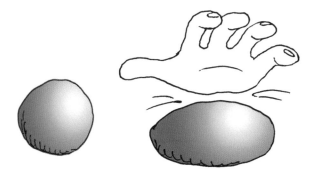

Make several ropes by making fat sausages of clay and rolling them on the table. When they are long enough curl them into rings like ring doughnuts.

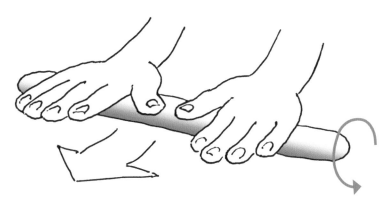

Using slip and an old tooth brush, roughen and soften the bottom of the first ring and the area it will be joined to on the base. Put the first ring on to the base. Smudge over the joins and prepare the next ring by brushing slip on to it. Add your next ring of clay and smudge it on.

As you add the clay rings and smooth over the joins you will pinch the clay together - a bit like thinning the walls of a thumb pot. In this way your pot will grow taller than the pile of rings it is made of.

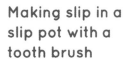

Making slip in a slip pot with a tooth brush

 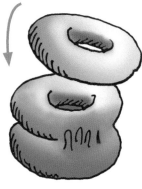 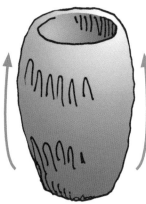

Base   **Rings of clay**   **Taller pot**

Building with Coils - Method 2

Make a ball of clay and flatten it for a base.

Using slip and an old tooth brush, roughen and soften the base where your coil is going to go. Make a longer sausage of clay and roll it on the table. When it is smooth and evenly thick take it and build a wall of clay on the base. Smudge over the joins. You can add more coils to make your pot taller. As with the first method, if you use a thick coil your pot will grow taller as you smudge and shape the clay into position.

The wall follows a "coil" shape, but it is really a **helix** - a helix is a spiral that rises in three dimensions rather than growing outwards in two dimensions.

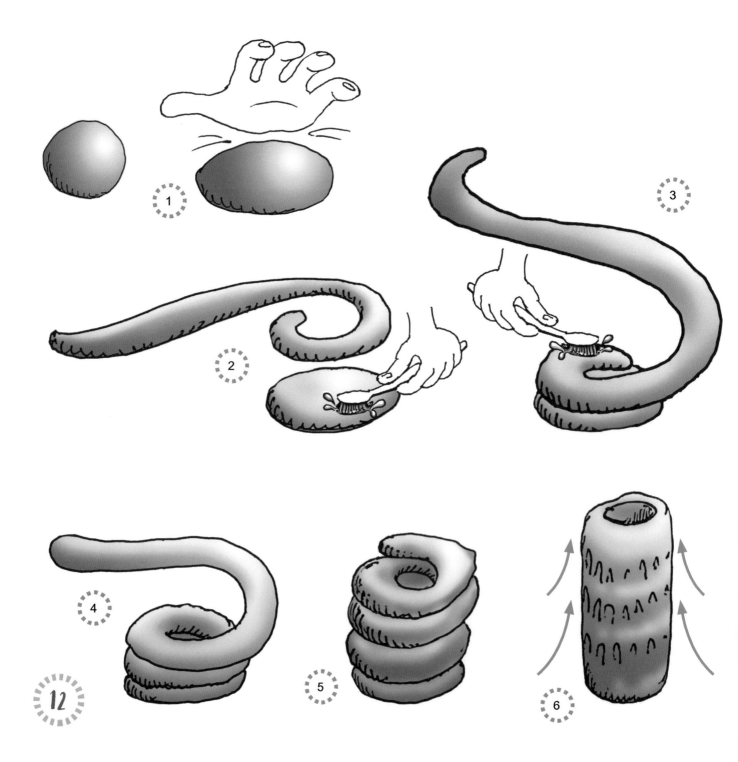

Building with Slabs

Take a large chunk of clay. Shape it into a brick by dropping it onto the table top, turning it over and dropping it again, until it is fairly squared off on all sides. Next flatten the brick of clay with your hands before finally using a rolling pin on it.

If your clay sticks to the table you can use a cloth or an old tea towel under the clay. Lift the cloth with the slab of clay and peel it off to release it. To get a really even slab of clay you can use guide sticks on each side to make the rolling pin give an even thickness.

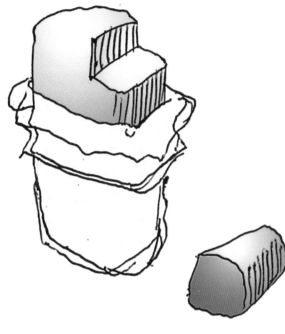

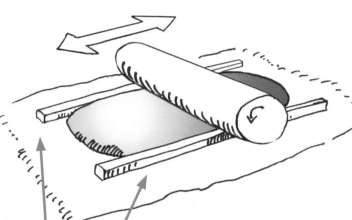

Guide sticks

Your slabs can be used to make many things with flat surfaces and curved to make cylindrical shapes like mugs, jugs and castle towers. You can also use paper templates to make more complex shapes.

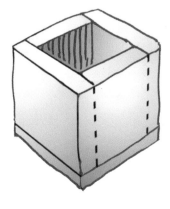

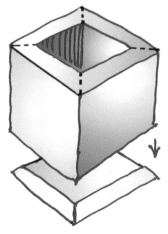

Slab built forms need to be carefully joined with slip to ensure they do not split along the seems on drying.

For box shapes you can use mitred corner joints to hide the joins along the edges. They are also slightly stronger than butted joints.

Butted joints   **Mitred joints**

Hollow Creatures

Suitable for making with fired clay **or** air drying clay

You can make larger things that will not crack when they dry by making them hollow. One way to do this is to make a solid sculpture and then cut it in half to carve out the middle, with a wire tool. This way the clay dries more evenly and will not split.

Another way is to make hollow shapes for the fat parts of your sculpture so that they will not need to be hollowed out later. An easy way to do this is to make two pinch pots of the same size and join them rim to rim.

Make a third smaller pinch pot for stirring up clay slip with a wetted tooth brush. Use the brush to apply the slip and score the surfaces to be joined at the same time. Then bring the two bowl shaped pinch pots together and smudge over the join area. Do this very thoroughly because you can not get to the inside to do any smudging together there.

Tap the rim of your pinch pots on the table to flatten the edges. This will help the two parts fit together well and increase the surface areas which touch in the join

Remember to make a hole to let moisture out as the clay dries

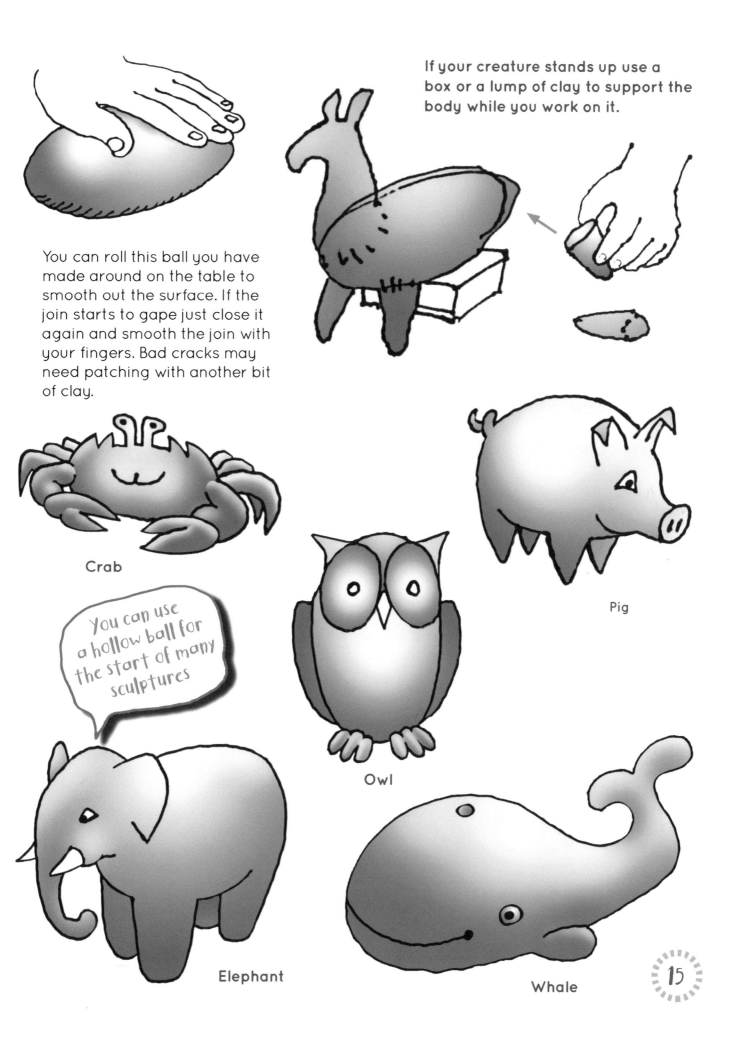

If your creature stands up use a box or a lump of clay to support the body while you work on it.

You can roll this ball you have made around on the table to smooth out the surface. If the join starts to gape just close it again and smooth the join with your fingers. Bad cracks may need patching with another bit of clay.

Crab

You can use a hollow ball for the start of many sculptures

Owl

Pig

Elephant

Whale

15

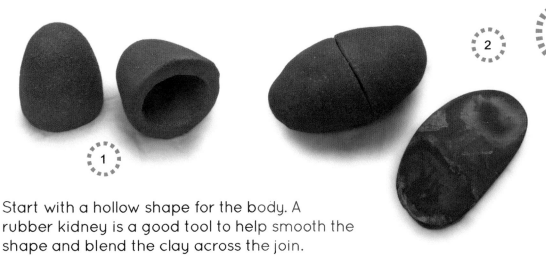

This project has been made with Crank Clay. It is very coarse which makes it suitable for chunky sculpture

Start with a hollow shape for the body. A rubber kidney is a good tool to help smooth the shape and blend the clay across the join.

When you are happy with the shape of the body make four equal sized pieces for the legs. A good way to do this is to roll a large coil of clay and cut it in half, then each half in half again.

Stand the body on a box or lump of clay at about the right height for your horse.

The legs are shaped before joining them to the body. Use plenty of slip and scratching of the surfaces to make a good join.

When the legs are done you can make the head and tail. The tail should be made long enough to stick it into a hole made in the body. Use a round paint brush handle to push a hole in, then fix the tail into the hole with slip. This will make the tail join much stronger than just fixing it to the surface of the horse's bottom.

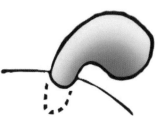

The head and neck is made from one solid piece of clay which is shaped before adding it to the model. Take some time to shape the bottom of the neck so that it will fit onto the curve of the shoulders. It is best to leave the eyes and ears until after the head is in position.

The ears are made from two tear drop shapes of clay and the eyes are little balls. You can get pairs of eyes and ears the same size by cutting a piece of clay in half with a knife as accurately as you can. If they are too big or small, start again with another piece of clay cut in half, bigger or smaller.

6

7

If you like you can give your horse a rider. This one is solid, made from a single piece of clay with added head, hands and feet.

If you are going to fire the horse in a kiln - Remember to make a hole in the hollow body before you let it dry

Other ideas

You can give your horse a bridle and saddle in clay, or cut a hole through the horses mouth for string reins.

Your rider does not have to be human! There could be a bird or animals on the horse's back.
You could make a cart for the horse to pull. The horse could have armour and be ridden by a knight.

The finished project is painted with underglaze and transparent glaze, fired to 1020°C

17

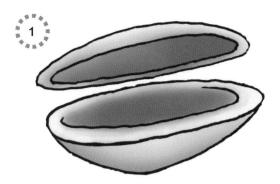

1

Two thumb pots for the body

Crab

This project has been made with Crank Clay.

You can make a small crab with a solid body. To make a giant crab you will need to make a hollow body. This model is not as difficult to make as it looks - as long as you support the weight of the crab and claws with small lumps of clay while the legs and claws are drying.

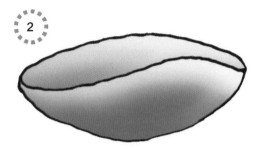

2

Hollow body

3

On the underside, socket holes for the crab's legs are made with a paint brush handle.

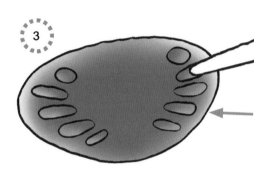

4

Rolling crab legs

5 Eyes

The crab's body is held up with a pad of clay like a cushion, while the legs dry. When the legs are strong the pad can be taken away, recycled and used for something else.

You also need to do this for the claws with taller clay supports.

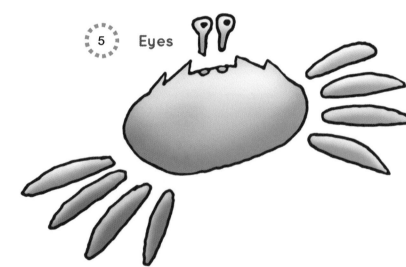

18

Clay Supports

6

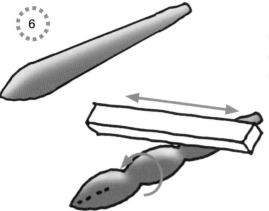

Pincers are made by dividing the claw with a knife or straight edge

The arms are given segments by rolling them with the edge of a stick

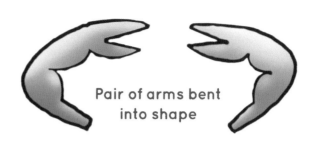

Pair of arms bent into shape

7

Claw pushed into socket hole in body

The finished crab has been biscuit fired and coloured with blue and black under-glazes. The blue has been painted into the cracks and hollows and then sponged away to emphasise the details of the sculpture. It has been painted with transparent glaze and fired to 1020°C.

With Air-hardening Clay you can use paint and varnish for the same look

A Mug with a Surprise

Suitable for making with fired clay

The frog inside the mug is completely hidden when you serve a drink in it. You can also make anything else you want to hide inside a mug. If you make the frog on a round base on its own, you can hide it in any shop-bought mug - which can be much more surprising!

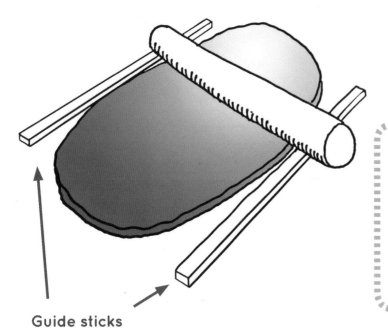

Guide sticks

Tools needed:
- Rolling pin
- Guide sticks
- Potters knife or other blunt knife
- Ruler
- Old tooth brush or paint brush
- Modelling tools

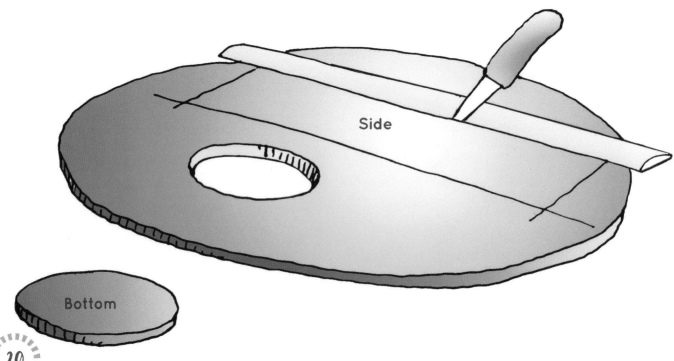

Side

Bottom

Mug Bits

Handle · Side · Bottom · Frog

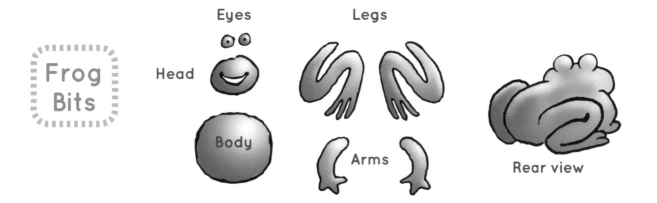

Frog Bits

Eyes · Legs · Head · Body · Arms · Rear view

Method:

Roll out a large slab of clay. Start with a block of soft clay and thump it down on the table to start it off, turning it over and throwing it down until it is thin enough to finish with a rolling pin.

Use some guide sticks if you want to get an even thickness. If your table top is shiny the clay may stick to it - if so, use a cloth to help you lift the clay off the table and turn it over. Do not make the slab of clay too thin to work with.

Cut a long rectangle of clay to be the body of the mug. Shape this into a cylinder. The size of your mug body will give you the size of the bottom you need to cut out. The easiest way to do this is to place your mug body onto the slab which is left over after taking the long rectangle to make the cylinder.

Model your surprise creature from solid clay - it does not need to be hollow and it does not have to be a frog. Take care, particularly with the eyes because it is the eyes which give your animal sculptures life.

Book Ends

Suitable for making with fired clay **and** air drying clay

Book ends are a fun way to keep your books stacked straight. Here are some ideas for book ends to make your book shelves much more interesting.

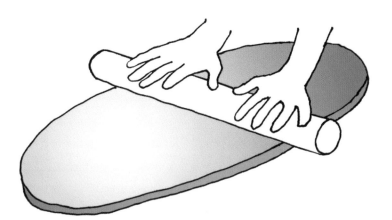

Start by rolling out some clay, about 14 inches long and 7 inches wide. Use a big piece of clay so that it can be half an inch thick.

Cut out a piece which is 6 inches wide by 12 inches long, using a ruler.

You can bend your clay into an "L" shape or cut it and use a mitred joint to make it very neat.

Prop your book end against a wall or use a biscuit tin on the table to support it while you add your sculpture to it.

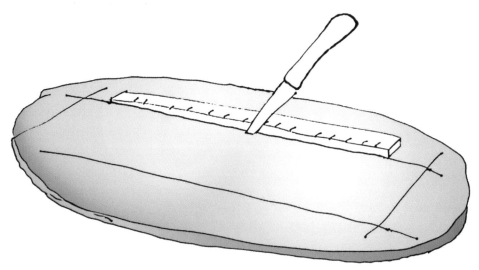

Remember: Use slip and scratching to join the things you make to the book end. All touching parts which you want to join need to be roughened and coated with slip so that they are squidgy before joining.

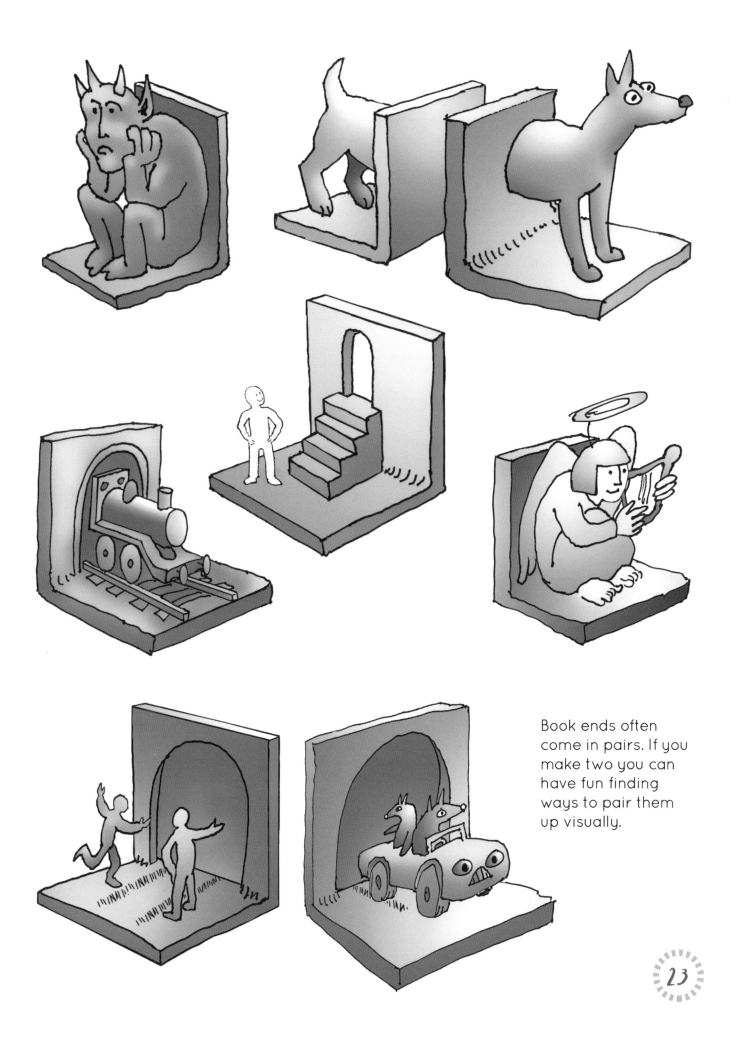

Book ends often come in pairs. If you make two you can have fun finding ways to pair them up visually.

23

Here is a pair of book ends with a dog split down the middle. The front end is made with a cone shaped thumb pot - it could also be made out of a slab cut and bent into a cone. Early on the head needs support with a chunk of clay to stop it drooping downwards. The legs are not hollow, they are made from turnip shaped pieces of clay which are smoothed onto the body.

The eyes are made from two small balls of clay stuck into hollows in the head. Then sausages of clay are added above and below the eye balls and blended into the head. This gives a realistic effect of the eyes being inside the head looking out - it looks better than eyes drawn onto the surface of the head.

The back end is also made out of a thumb pot with solid clay legs and tail added to it. The tail is a small lump of clay rolled into a sausage shape.

It is easier to keep the book end slabs straight if they are thicker!

To make sure the tail will stay on, a hole is pushed into the dogs bottom with a paint brush handle. Then the tail and hole can be roughened and wetted with a tooth brush, so the tail can be stuck into the hole and joined really well.

The book end slabs are a bit thin in these pictures, fatter slabs are much easier to work with.

When you finish off your book ends remember that they will be coming into close contact with books. This means all the surfaces which will touch the books should be very smooth.

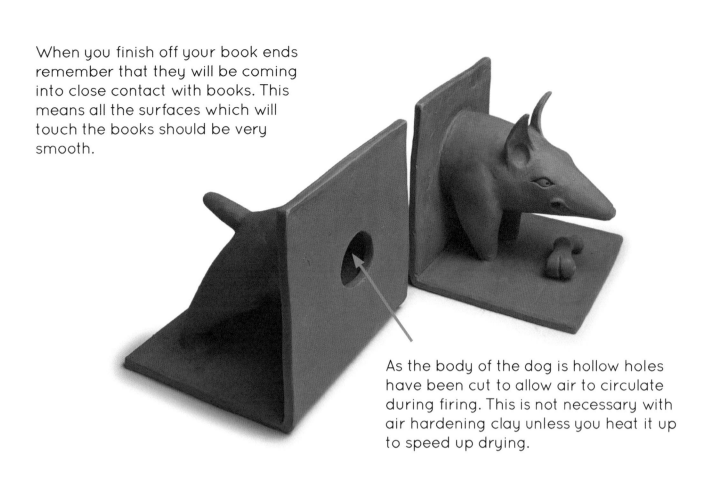

As the body of the dog is hollow holes have been cut to allow air to circulate during firing. This is not necessary with air hardening clay unless you heat it up to speed up drying.

GRRRRR!!!

Hard clay feels much sharper than soft clay. Smooth the edges carefully while clay is soft.

Name Plates

Suitable for making with fired clay

A name plate on the door of your room, or words on your wall can express your personality. Here is a way to make them with coloured glass.

First roll out a slab of clay and sketch the letters of your name or another word you like by drawing with your finger. This gives you the chance to get the proportions right - smooth it out with a rubber kidney and do it again if it doesn't look right.

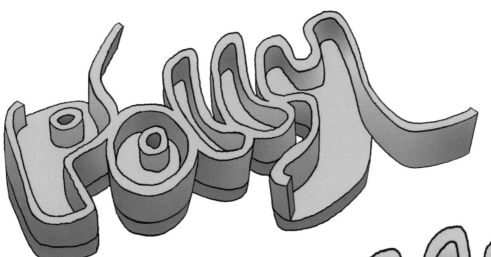

Then take another flat slab and cut it into strips. The strips will form low walls to put around the edges of the sketched letters.

Make sure the walls are well fixed down and seal the joins. Any holes will allow molten glass to spill onto the kiln shelf.

Biscuit fire the word you have made when it is thoroughly dry. It can then be painted with underglaze colours and a coating of transparent glaze. Place coloured glass marbles into each letter shape. These will melt in a biscuit firing of 1000°C.

You can also use sea glass collected on the beach or recycle coloured glass bottles.

Be very careful if you break the glass!

This word was made to go on the cover of this book. Some of the marbles were put into a sack and broken with a hammer to make them fit. If you make big letters you will not have to do this.

27

Tower Houses

Suitable for making with fired clay **and** air drying clay

This is a slab building project - *see page 13.* Model buildings can be made taller if you build rooms on their own, ready to be stacked later when they are dry.

Each room is a box with a floor. The ground floor can be built on a larger slab of clay. The roof can be sloped or left flat with a wall around the edges, like a castle tower so that people can stand and look out.

Inside the boxes there is space to build stairs and cut holes for trap doors.

You can easily make two flights of stairs from a thick slab of clay - just cut a square slab and divide it diagonally as shown, with a zig zag edge.

Everything is made from slabs of clay except for the birds and the small person on the balcony.

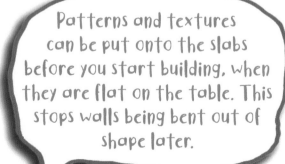

Patterns and textures can be put onto the slabs before you start building, when they are flat on the table. This stops walls being bent out of shape later.

When you put the birds onto the roof it is good to make the feet first, out of balls of clay, and fix them to the ridge. Then use slip and plenty of scratching to stick the birds onto the foot shaped pads of clay.

Bird Bits

Roof Bits

The balcony is made by carefully cutting an arched doorway into a wall of the first storey. The piece that comes out of this doorway is placed horizontally to make the balcony, as shown below. Make a wall or balustrade so that people wont fall off.

Then you can make a figure which is the right size to be stood on the balcony. It is more fun if you do not stick figures down so that you can re-position them later.

Attic

Balcony Bits

First Floor

Steps can be made so that they fit into corners.

Ground Floor

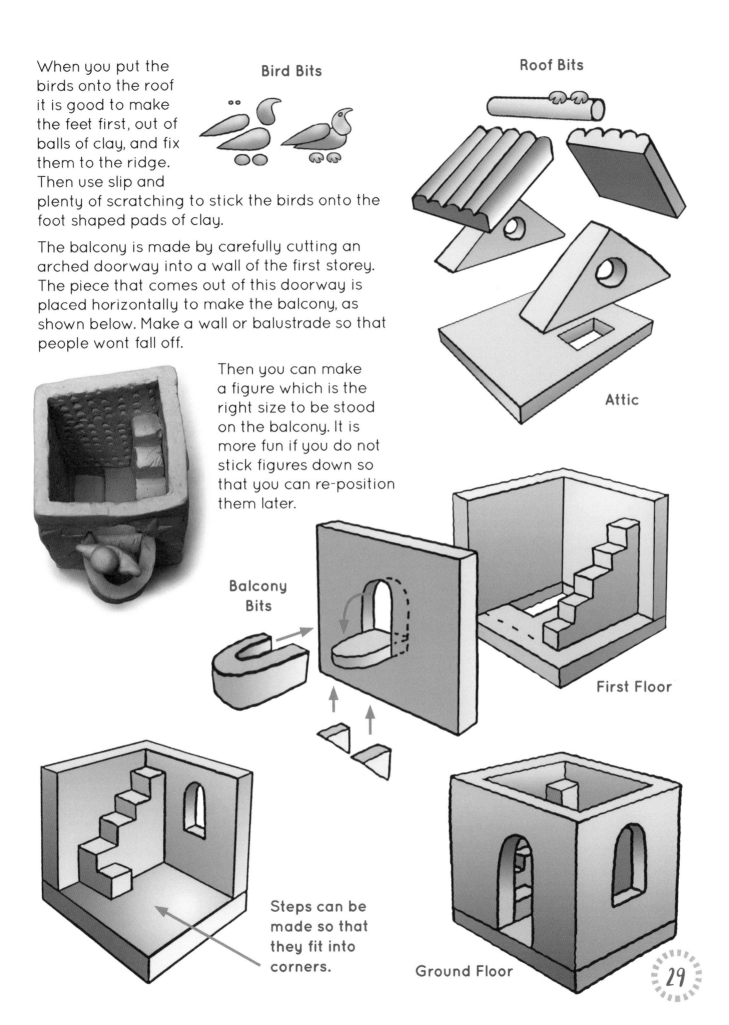

Painting & Glazing

If you are using air-hardenning clay you can paint with poster paint. Mix it with PVA to get a better bond and slightly shiny finish, or use PVA as a varnish. If using underglaze and glaze before glaze firing the painting technique is the same. The difference is you have to fire the piece again before it is finished and you can see the colours through the glaze.

With detailed surfaces, like the walls of this house, it is good to paint into the cracks and patterns and then sponge it off again for a heightened texture effect. This can be done with both paint, for air hardened clay, or underglaze colour for fired clay. Apply the colour thinned with water so that it gets into all the nooks and crannies, then take a damp sponge and wipe colour off the highlights. - This is easier to achieve with biscuit fired clay as it does not get muddy again when wet.

The final coating of brush on glaze should be applied thickly with two or three coats to get good coverage. If glaze is two thin it will be less shiny and more patchy in appearance after firing.

With air hardening clay, finishing with a PVA coating will strengthen the surface as well as bring out the colours of the paints.

This house has been painted with underglaze paints and brush on transparent glaze - fired to 1020°C.

The house can be rotated into different positions and if you want to make more parts to stack, the sky is the limit.

Can you think of any more architectural features to add to your house?

Wonderful Panoramic views from up here.

Welcome to my moving house!

Things with Tea Lights

Suitable for making with fired clay **and** air drying clay

Clay can be used to make candle holders of many different sorts. If you do not want to use a live flame candle, LED candles that run on small batteries can be used instead.

The simplest ones to make are also some of the most beautiful. Using a thumb pot as a starting point, make a dome big enough to cover a tea light candle. By piercing this dome light is let out into a darkened room, throwing patterns onto walls and ceiling.

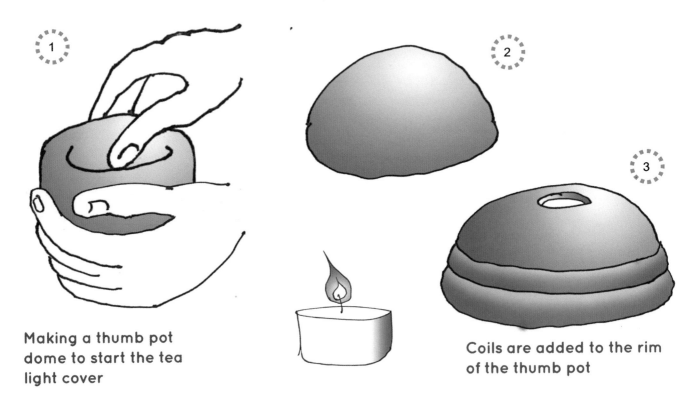

Making a thumb pot dome to start the tea light cover

Coils are added to the rim of the thumb pot

The dome is smoothed and thinned before any holes are cut. The holes can be any shape you like. You could try making star shaped holes with a pointed knife, or use a hole cutter or metal drinking straw to poke out round holes. Make sure to leave a larger hole over the candle if you are going to use a live flame.

Hole to let heat out

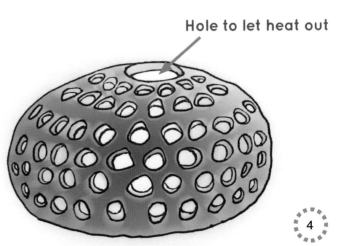

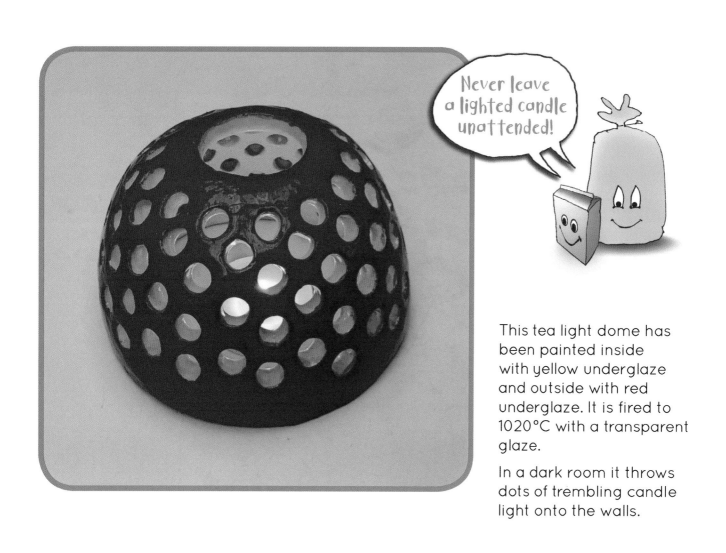

This tea light dome has been painted inside with yellow underglaze and outside with red underglaze. It is fired to 1020°C with a transparent glaze.

In a dark room it throws dots of trembling candle light onto the walls.

More Light Ideas

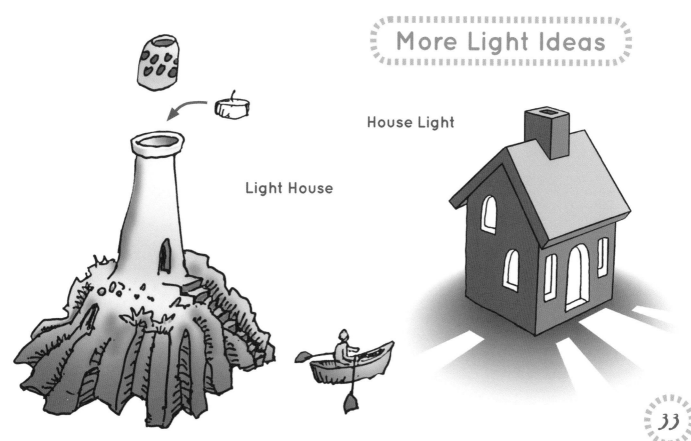

Light House

House Light

33

Camp Fire Light

1 - The mound for the camp fire is made by smoothing a rolled slab of clay into a shallow bowl using a rubber kidney tool.

2 - The shape is then trimmed with a knife to level the edge which will be the at the bottom.

3 - When it is leather hard, the clay is turned out of the mould and a circular hole is cut so that a small cup for the candle can be inserted.

4 - The round disc of clay which was taken from the hole is used as the base of the candle holder cup.

5 - The cup is fitted back into the hole, which has been carefully prepared for joining with slip, and a lump of clay is used to support the cup in position while it dries.

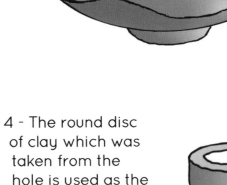

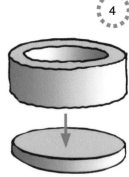

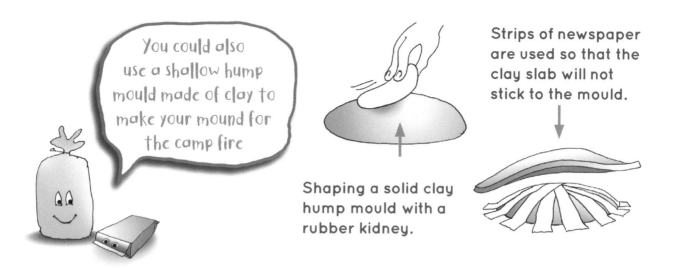

You could also use a shallow hump mould made of clay to make your mound for the camp fire

Shaping a solid clay hump mould with a rubber kidney.

Strips of newspaper are used so that the clay slab will not stick to the mould.

The camp fire and figure have been left unglazed. After biscuit firing, red iron oxide has been washed on with a soft brush and water, and then rubbed back with a damp sponge. Then they were fired again to 980°C in the next biscuit firing, to fix the colour.

The Camp Fire candle holder is very stable

Clay Whistles

Suitable for making with fired clay and air drying clay

There is something magical about making your piece of clay play a musical note.

1 - 3 Make two small thumb pots and join them rim to rim, to make a hollow ball.

4 - 6 Make a tapering wad of clay for the mouth piece, shaped so that it can be joined to the hollow ball.

7 Join the mouth piece to the ball with little or no added moisture so that you can push a hole through it which will not be too soggy. Use your clean lolly stick to push a hole down the mouth piece right into the hollow ball.

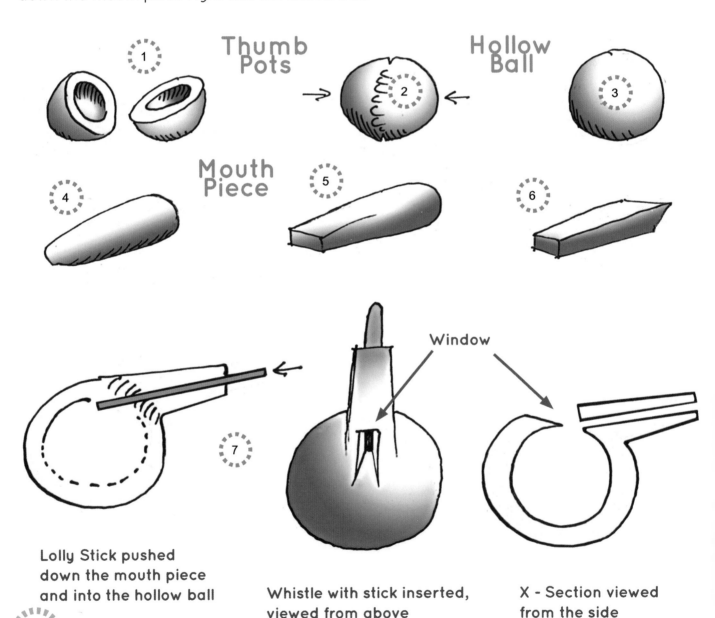

Thumb Pots

Hollow Ball

Mouth Piece

Window

Lolly Stick pushed down the mouth piece and into the hollow ball

Whistle with stick inserted, viewed from above

X - Section viewed from the side

With the lolly stick in place, use your knife to cut a window down to the stick as illustrated. This window should have a sharp edge where the blown air strikes it - like an organ pipe or penny whistle. See diagrams.

Make sure that it is as clean as a whistle before you attempt to blow a note. More notes can be obtained by making small holes in the ball, you can place these holes so that they lie under your fingers when holding the whistle. The notes can be tuned relative to each other by altering the size of the holes.

This whistle creature has been made from coarse crank clay

Coat Hooks

It is very important to make good joins on these!

Suitable for making with fired clay

Your coat hooks can be both functional and fun. Fired clay is strong enough to be screwed to a wall or door, so why not make your own Coat Hooks?

Starting with the back plate, which can be made from a squashed ball of clay, make an upside down keyhole shaped opening to fix the hook to the wall or door. This hole will fit over a screw head and then slide down snugly. Use the screw you intend to use to get the hole and slot big enough, allowing for shrinkage.

Use your imagination to build a unique coat hook - it can be an animal or bird or anything else that has a shape which can take a hat or coat. Or use one of these ideas to get started.

The back plate is given a hole ready for hanging before the head is in place

This small rhino head started as a thumb pot, then the horn was added

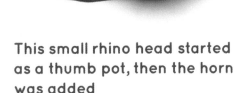

Here the parts to be joined have been scored and well moistened with clay slip before they are pressed together

It is important to seal the joins very well so that cracks do not appear between the head and the back plate as they dry

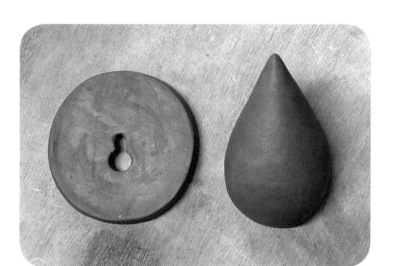

This bird shaped coat hook starts as a pointed pinch pot. A discus shaped piece of clay is divided to make wings. Each wing is shaped to fit the body of the bird before joining.

Rounded dents are made on the head to take the eye balls.

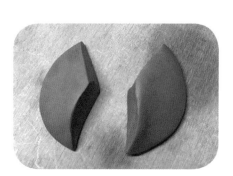

Once they are fired, and glazed if you wish, the hooks can be fixed to a wall or door by hanging them on a screw. The screw should be left protruding just enough to let the back plate slide down over it.

Here are some more ideas for coat hooks

The finished bird hook

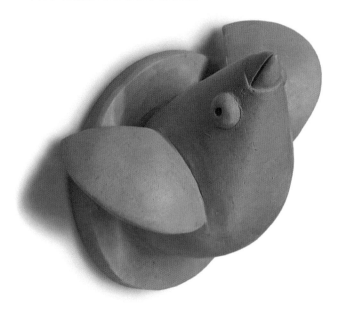

The bird hook painted with underglaze colours and fired with transparent glaze to 1020°C.

Back plate   **Elephant Head**   **Elephant Hook**

Things with Wheels

Suitable for making with fired clay **and** air drying clay

Bamboo skewers make very good axles for things with wheels. You can get them from most super markets as they are commonly used for making kebabs for the barbecue.

Just remember that clay **shrinks** as it dries - if you leave soft clay skewered on bamboo it will be difficult to get it off without breaking it when it is dry. This means that freely moving parts need to be fairly loose to fit back onto a skewer after firing.

You can make a huge range of vehicles out of clay, from cars to toast racks.

Wheels can be made from balls of clay.

1. Make a set of four balls of clay, all the same size.

2. Roll them on the table so that they become cylindrical.

3. Take a pen top or other round thing to make a circular dent on one side. This step is optional but can look good.

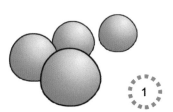

4. Use a thin paint brush handle or bamboo skewer to make a hole through the middle of the wheel.
    - This is more easily done by rolling the wheel along the table as you insert the skewer.

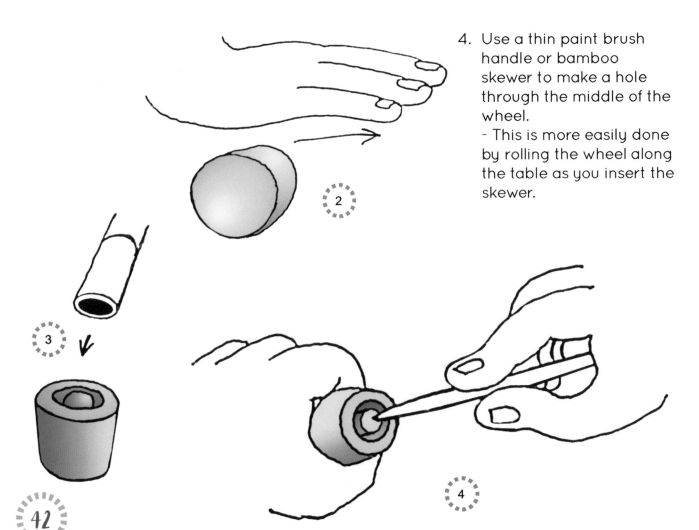

Toast Rack

This is fairly simple to make but be sure your wheels have enough space under the base to turn.

1. Make five dividers out of rounded slabs of clay - these should be slightly smaller than your toast - and one larger slab for the base of your toast rack.

2. Add two thick walls of clay to the base. These will be underneath to take the bamboo skewer axles.

3. Make holes through the walls with a paint brush handle which is thicker than your skewers.

4. Slice the rounded bottoms off the dividers so they can be joined to the top of the flat base.

5. Make wheels as shown previously.

6. Cut a hole in one end of the base to attach a string and make a bead to be attached to the string as a handle.

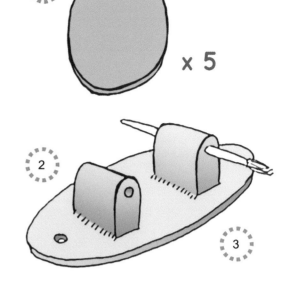

x 5

Holes for axles must be loose fitting for wheels to roll.

x 5

The finished roller toast rack has been painted with underglaze colour and glazed with transparent glaze. It has a nylon cord and polymer clay bead handle.

43

Skate
boarder
cat

The cat has been painted with blue underglaze which has been rubbed back with a sponge. The skateboard has thickly painted underglaze. The wheels are painted with a layer of green and then a layer of blue underglaze.

All have a layer of transparent glaze fired to 1020°C

44

Joy rider dogs

Faster! Faster!

Car - showing the axle holes under the wheel arches

Page 54

Page 52

Page 58

Page 60

Page 59

Page 56

Page 64

Polymer Clay Basics

Polymer clay has the great advantage of being brightly coloured from the start and the clay body reaches a mature fused state at much more manageable temperatures than ceramic clay. This is because it is made of very finely grained plastic granules, colours and fillers with mineral oil - unlike dug clay, which is finely grained alumina and silica with water.

Polymer clay can be conserved in a sealed plastic bag after it has been opened. A resealable freezer bag is good. It dries much more slowly than natural clay as it has no water to evaporate.

Tools

Most of the tools that you need can be found in your home. Get ready by collecting them together.

- Clay modelling tools for shaping
- A small rolling pin or length of dowel
- Aluminium foil
- Grease proof paper
- Lolly sticks or craft sticks
- Toothpicks
- Paper clips

You will also need an oven and a flat baking tray for hardening your projects in the oven.

Using Polymer Clay

- Work Area: Clear a space on a table and use grease proof paper to work on. This will stop your work from sticking to the table top. Polymer clay can be a little oily and can stain wooden surfaces.

- Warm Up: Before the polymer clay is fully workable it needs a work out. Condition the clay by rolling it around in your hands and squeezing it between your fingers. A ball of polymer should not crack when it is squashed into a disc. If you do not do this before you start, your project may crack open during baking.

- Keep Colours Clean: Washing your hands between warming up different colours will help to keep the colours clean. It is very easy for little bits of polymer on your hands to be transferred between colours. Once the polymer clay is warmed up it sticks to your hands more easily. A little bit of hand cream rubbed into your hands and fingers will help stop this from happening.

- Be Creative with Colour: If you need a colour you have not got you can mix a new colour from different colour clays. Knead it thoroughly for a smooth colour or leave it streaky for a marbled effect. Coils of different colours can be rolled across each other for a Barber's Pole effect. The secondary colours; green, purple and orange are always brighter if they are not mixed from two primary colours but come straight from a packet. A bright purple is particularly difficult to mix from red and blue. However, you can make some very subtle colours by mixing. Flesh tones can be best achieved by mixing colours.

Colour Blends

It is a good idea to visually measure the colours you blend. Equal amounts of yellow and blue will give a mid-green. Blends of colour can be left with veins running through or more thoroughly blended for a smooth single colour.

Twisting two coils together is a quick way to thoroughly blend their colours.

Colour Wheel

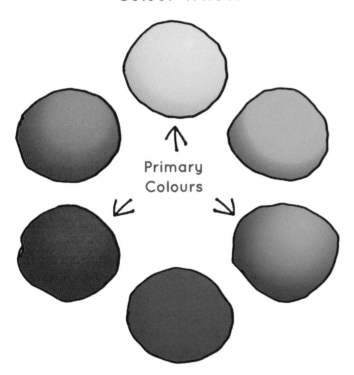

Primary Colours

The colour wheel shows the three primary colours with the secondary colours blended between them

Marbled

Smooth

- Joining parts of a project is easy if the polymer is well warmed up. Polymer clay is naturally sticky before it is baked. If your polymer clay gets a little dried out after storing it for a long time, it can be revitalised with a small amount of mineral oil. A small dab of mineral oil can also help with joining polymer clay parts.

- You can collect useful tools for your projects and keep them in a box. Many different tools can be used for shaping and cutting polymer clay and you do not have to buy special tools. Tooth picks are useful for poking holes through beads and shaping small parts. Clean lolly sticks make good modelling tools. If you use knives and teaspoons from the kitchen, keep them separate from the ones you use for food.

- Different polymer clay manufacturers produce products which mature at different temperatures, so always use the instructions which come with your polymer clay when baking your projects. An adult should always be present to supervise the use of an oven. Baked polymer can be hot enough to burn hands when it first comes out of the oven.

- Use grease proof paper on a flat baking tray to bake your polymer projects. Delicate pieces can be supported with aluminium foil to stop them sagging in the oven.

Graduated Colour Blends

You can get good graduated colour effects with methodically blended colours.

Method

1. Tear off two equal sized lumps of differing colours of polymer and knead until conditioned.

2. Roll into equal length coils and place side by side.

3. Mark out divisions of ascending size - roughly increase by a third to the size of each division as you go up.

4. Cut and arrange the pieces back to front, so that the longest piece of one coil is matched with the shortest of the other, and so on.

5. Blend these pairs into balls of well kneaded polymer.

6. Squash the balls and stack them in order.

7. Compress and shape the stack into a block.

8. Slice the block with a sharp knife to reveal the colour blend.

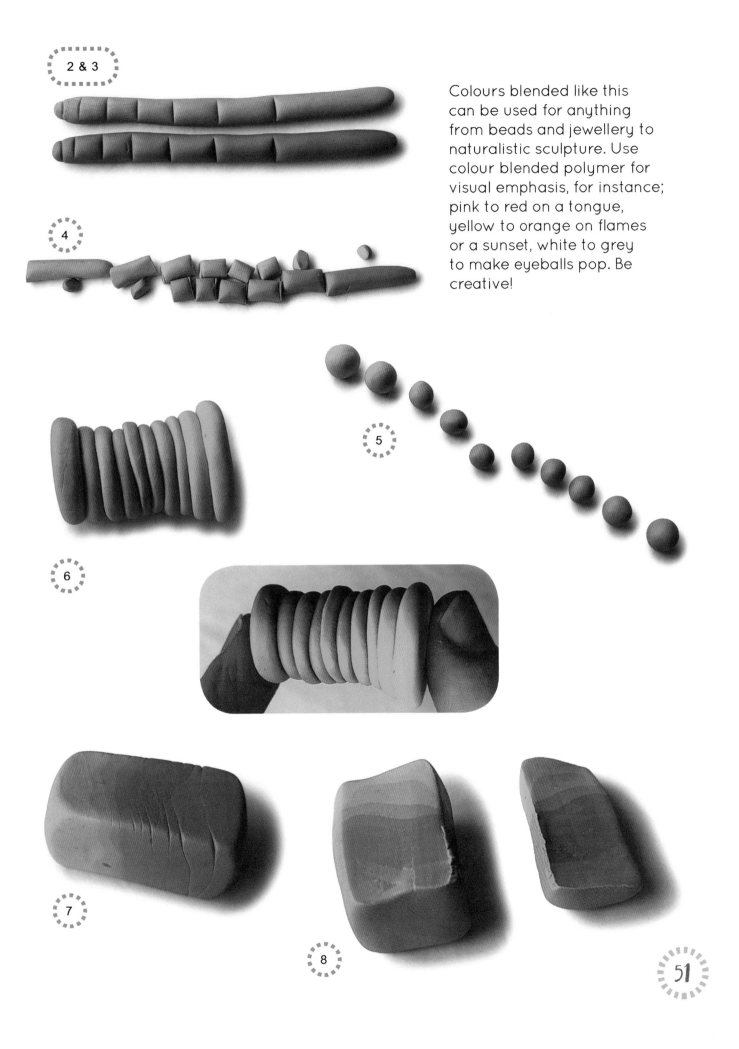

2 & 3

4

Colours blended like this can be used for anything from beads and jewellery to naturalistic sculpture. Use colour blended polymer for visual emphasis, for instance; pink to red on a tongue, yellow to orange on flames or a sunset, white to grey to make eyeballs pop. Be creative!

5

6

7

8

Pulls for Lights & Blinds

Suitable for making with polymer clay

Many houses have light switches with a string hanging from the ceiling, or window blinds which get pulled down. They often have plain plastic pullers at the bottom which are light enough not to do any damage to walls or windows if they swing around. This sounds like an ideal candidate for polymer clay customisation!

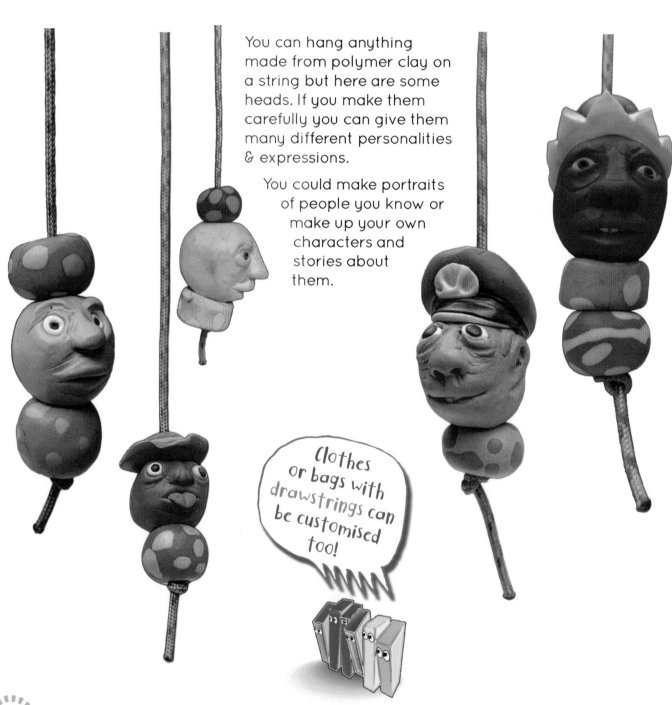

You can hang anything made from polymer clay on a string but here are some heads. If you make them carefully you can give them many different personalities & expressions.

You could make portraits of people you know or make up your own characters and stories about them.

Clothes or bags with drawstrings can be customised too!

52

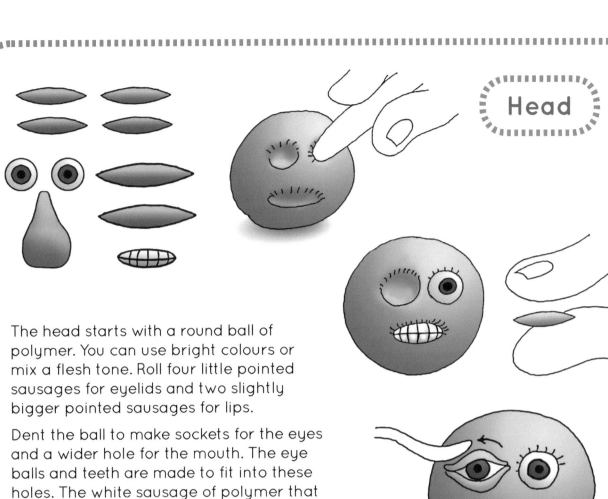

The head starts with a round ball of polymer. You can use bright colours or mix a flesh tone. Roll four little pointed sausages for eyelids and two slightly bigger pointed sausages for lips.

Dent the ball to make sockets for the eyes and a wider hole for the mouth. The eye balls and teeth are made to fit into these holes. The white sausage of polymer that goes into the mouth can be marked with a knife or sharp modelling tool to divide it into separate teeth. Alternatively a tongue can be made to fit in the mouth.

The eyelids & lips are placed carefully and smoothed into position. You can use your fingers or a rounded modelling tool for this.

The nose is added and given nostrils by inserting a skewer or paint brush handle. Flare the nostrils for an indignant or angry expression.

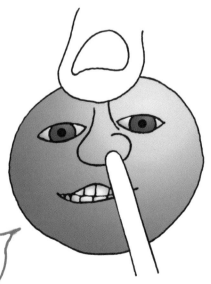

Why haven't I got any ears?

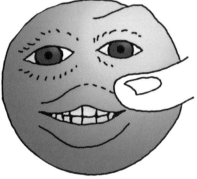

Do not forget to make a hole down the middle to thread them before they are baked.

Pencil Toppers

Suitable for making with polymer clay

Polymer clay is perfect for making bright coloured pencil toppers for your pens and pencils. You could make themed sets of animals, fruit, space craft, planets or any other thing which can be made in miniature and stuck on a pencil.

Here are some to get you started. Each one has a picture to show the parts which are needed and how they go together. You should use the sharp end of a pencil to start the hole and then make it bigger with the blunt end so that the pencil will slide in easily.

If you are having trouble getting parts to stick together you can use a little mineral oil to make the surfaces stickier.

If

Unicorn

The unicorn is simple to make because it is just the neck and head of the animal. The ears can be shaped with a toothpick to give them a hollow on the inside. The horn is made by twisting two worms of different colours of rolled polymer together. These are then rolled on the table to make a cone shaped horn and cut neatly across at the fat end before being added to the head.

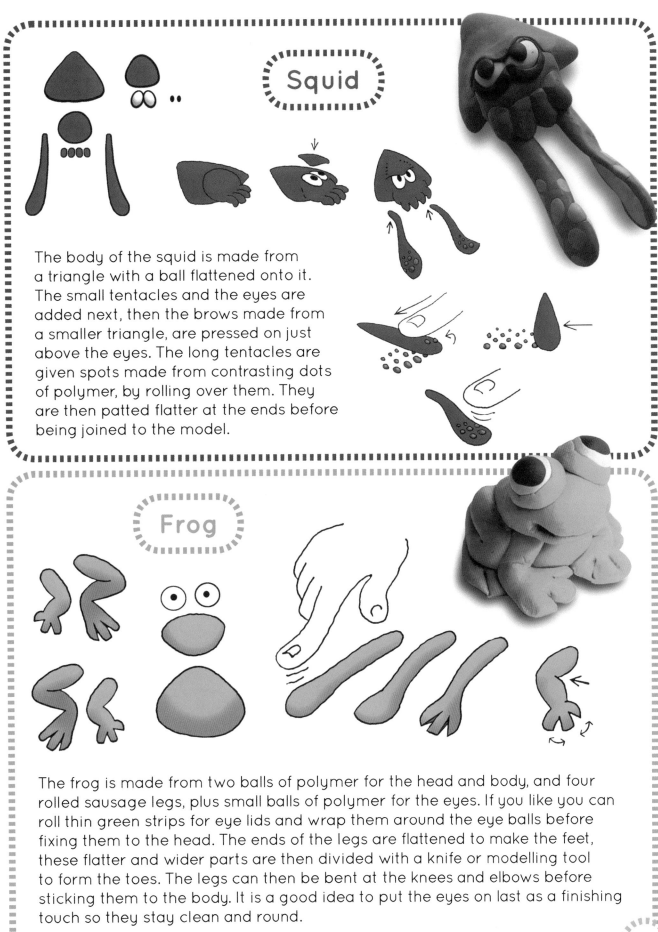

Squid

The body of the squid is made from a triangle with a ball flattened onto it. The small tentacles and the eyes are added next, then the brows made from a smaller triangle, are pressed on just above the eyes. The long tentacles are given spots made from contrasting dots of polymer, by rolling over them. They are then patted flatter at the ends before being joined to the model.

Frog

The frog is made from two balls of polymer for the head and body, and four rolled sausage legs, plus small balls of polymer for the eyes. If you like you can roll thin green strips for eye lids and wrap them around the eye balls before fixing them to the head. The ends of the legs are flattened to make the feet, these flatter and wider parts are then divided with a knife or modelling tool to form the toes. The legs can then be bent at the knees and elbows before sticking them to the body. It is a good idea to put the eyes on last as a finishing touch so they stay clean and round.

Fridge Magnets

Suitable for making with polymer clay

Polymer clay is ideal for making fridge magnets because it is light and brightly coloured. You can make them in almost any shape so long as they are flat on the back to glue on a strong magnet. Here are some ice cream fridge magnets made by adults and children. You can make many different toppings for polymer ice creams. Syrup can be moulded into drips and added on top. "Hundreds of Thousands" sprinkles can be made by rolling different colours very thin and cutting them into tiny pieces.

Blending the colours can give good ice cream effects too. A ripple effect can be made by rolling thin worms and twisting them together before rolling the mixture into a ball.

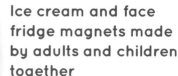

Mmmm!

Ice cream and face fridge magnets made by adults and children together

56

Mixing colour for ice cream cones from red, yellow and grey polymer.

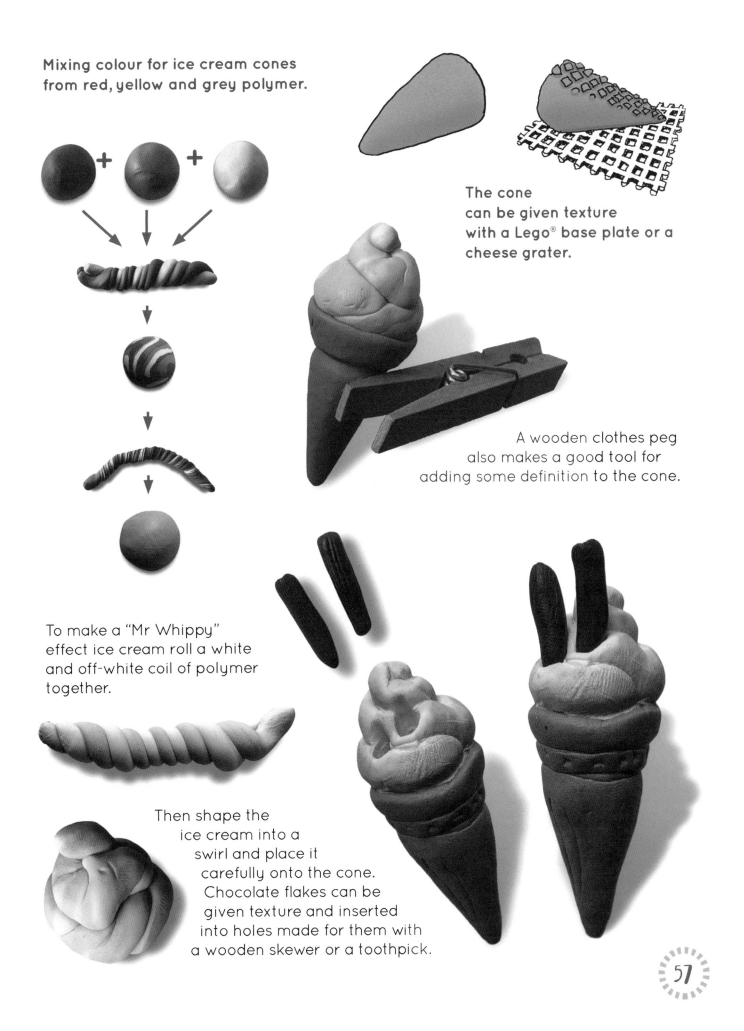

The cone can be given texture with a Lego® base plate or a cheese grater.

A wooden clothes peg also makes a good tool for adding some definition to the cone.

To make a "Mr Whippy" effect ice cream roll a white and off-white coil of polymer together.

Then shape the ice cream into a swirl and place it carefully onto the cone. Chocolate flakes can be given texture and inserted into holes made for them with a wooden skewer or a toothpick.

Millefiori Buttons

Suitable for making with polymer clay

The term millefiori is a combination of the Italian words "mille" (thousand) and "fiori" (flowers). It makes extremely detailed decoration by stretching coloured material which has been stacked to make patterned blocks. The blocks become long and thin and are called Millefiori Canes. The technique comes from Italian glassware, where stretched glass canes are sliced up to make colourful beads and larger bowls and vases. The ancient Romans made millefiori glass two thousand years ago and the technique remains the same.

Here is a millefiori pattern block being made from coils of polymer clay.

The block is squeezed together and then stretched by rolling to make it long and thin.

Then the cane is sliced like salami to make the patterned discs which will be buttons.

Use of sharp tools like knives should be supervised by an adult!

Rolling the cane as it is cut

Round buttons

Slicing up millefiori canes requires a sharp knife to get a clean cut.

The best way to cut the cane and keep the buttons round is to roll the cane under the knife as you cut. If you want to make square buttons this does not matter so much.

The round buttons are cut as thin as possible and then squashed a bit more to get them to the required thinness. They reveal the inner pattern of the cane.

The square buttons are cut longer and squashed sideways on to show the outside pattern of the cane.

Finally the buttons are given holes for sewing with a toothpick or bamboo skewer.

Square buttons

Blended green buttons

Handles For Spoons

Suitable for making with polymer clay

Stainless steel teaspoons are ideal for customisation with polymer clay. You can personalise spoons for family members or make themed sets. Any metal cutlery will do but teaspoons are small enough to be given handles without using up too much polymer. Here are Leopard and an Okapi spoon handles.

Leopard Spoon

To make the Leopard spoon handle:

1 - Choose a bright orange/brown to be your base colour and roll it into a 150mm sausage about 5mm thick. Wind this around the handle in an ascending spiral and smooth it out by pressing it on, so that the ridges merge together.

It is good to use a plain spoon with a straight narrow handle

2 - When the base colour is smooth add the leopard markings - these are called *rosettes.*

They are made from balls of polymer flattened onto the handle, first a ball of toffee colour followed by three dots of dark chocolate brown.

3 - Gently press the coloured balls down so they lie flat in the surface of the handle. Then with a clean piece of paper on the table top, press out any remaining bumps and re-shape the handle using the flat surface of the table as a shaping tool. The rosettes will become a little distorted, which makes them look more natural.

4 - Finally, finish off the handle with a collar of contrasting colour made from a fine coil of polymer.

You are now ready to bake your spoon in the oven following the instructions on the polymer clay packet.

This handle is NOT Dishwasher Safe!

To make the Okapi spoon handle:

1 - Roll dark grey and white sausages of polymer, then slice them into chunks. The chunks get smaller or larger from right to left.

2 - Combine the chunks into one longer sausage and squeeze them together. Rolling the combined sausage on the table gives it a regular shape - it also distorts the stripes of coloured polymer making a more random pattern.

3 - Use a screwdriver or skewer to start a hole in the polymer handle. This is where the teaspoon handle will be pushed in.

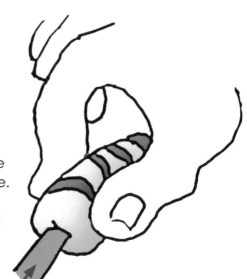

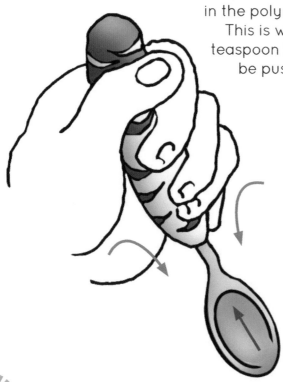

4 - Then slide the polymer handle onto the spoon handle. You may have to shove it hard.

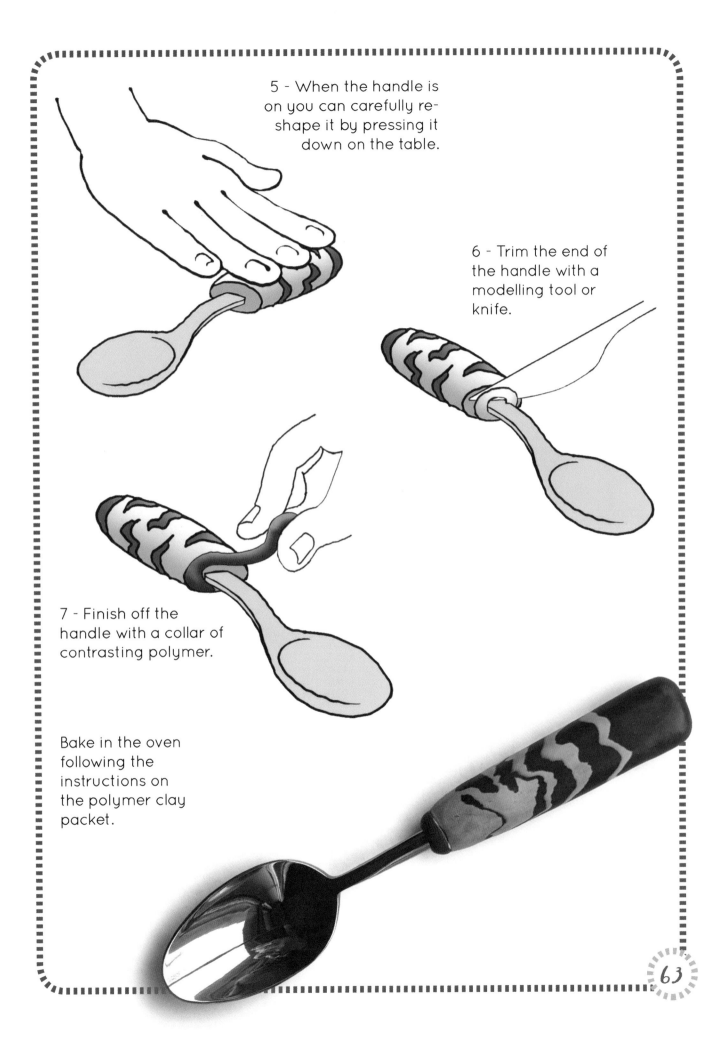

5 - When the handle is on you can carefully re-shape it by pressing it down on the table.

6 - Trim the end of the handle with a modelling tool or knife.

7 - Finish off the handle with a collar of contrasting polymer.

Bake in the oven following the instructions on the polymer clay packet.

Bugs and Beasties

Suitable for making with polymer clay

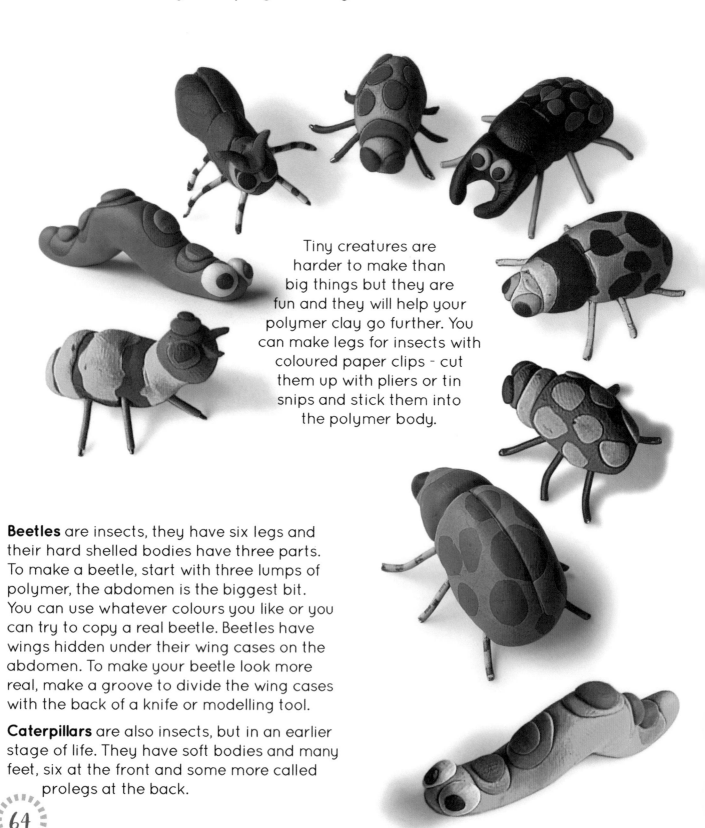

Tiny creatures are harder to make than big things but they are fun and they will help your polymer clay go further. You can make legs for insects with coloured paper clips - cut them up with pliers or tin snips and stick them into the polymer body.

Beetles are insects, they have six legs and their hard shelled bodies have three parts. To make a beetle, start with three lumps of polymer, the abdomen is the biggest bit. You can use whatever colours you like or you can try to copy a real beetle. Beetles have wings hidden under their wing cases on the abdomen. To make your beetle look more real, make a groove to divide the wing cases with the back of a knife or modelling tool.

Caterpillars are also insects, but in an earlier stage of life. They have soft bodies and many feet, six at the front and some more called prolegs at the back.

Abdomen   Thorax   Head

Beetle

The legs are added at the end. Bend them into shape before sticking them in.

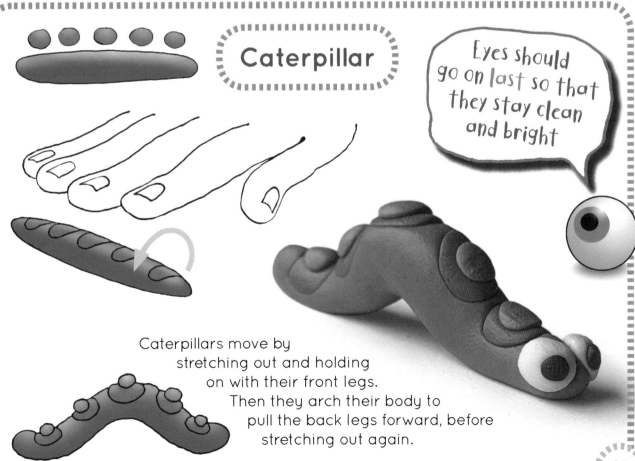

Caterpillar

Eyes should go on last so that they stay clean and bright

Caterpillars move by stretching out and holding on with their front legs. Then they arch their body to pull the back legs forward, before stretching out again.

Part Three - Multi-Clay

The following pages contain some projects that can be made with all three types of clay. The last one, **Pirate Gold**, is only possible if you combine the different qualities of natural clay and polymer clay to make stamp tools to mint polymer clay coins.

Page 74

Page 68

Page 80

Page 76

Page 78

Plant Pot Wildlife

Suitable for making with fired clay, air drying clay **and polymer clay**

Small birds and animals to turn your house plants into a tropical scene.

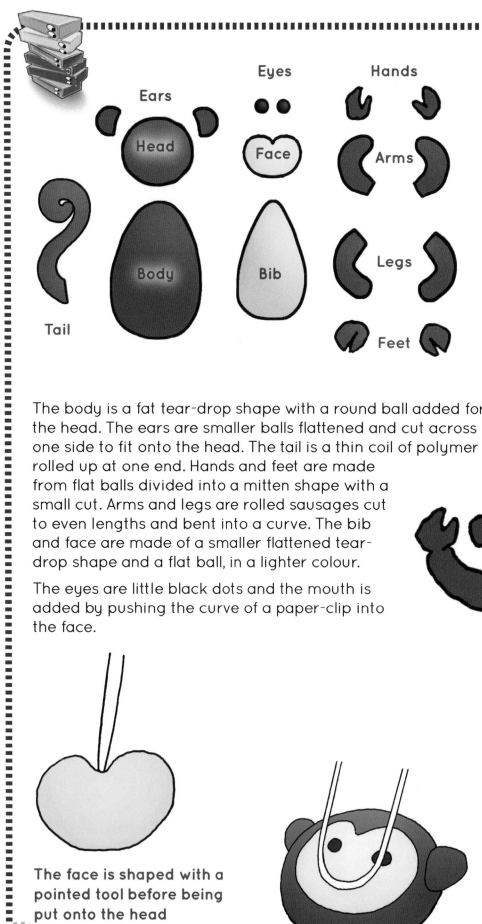

Ears

Eyes

Hands

Head

Face

Arms

Body

Bib

Legs

Tail

Feet

Monkey

The monkey is made from tear-drop shapes, balls and sausages of brown and pale peach polymer.

Little bits of tooth pick can be used inside the arms and legs to make joins stronger.

The body is a fat tear-drop shape with a round ball added for the head. The ears are smaller balls flattened and cut across one side to fit onto the head. The tail is a thin coil of polymer rolled up at one end. Hands and feet are made from flat balls divided into a mitten shape with a small cut. Arms and legs are rolled sausages cut to even lengths and bent into a curve. The bib and face are made of a smaller flattened tear-drop shape and a flat ball, in a lighter colour.

The eyes are little black dots and the mouth is added by pushing the curve of a paper-clip into the face.

The face is shaped with a pointed tool before being put onto the head

A paper-clip being used to add a curved mouth to the face

70

Parrot

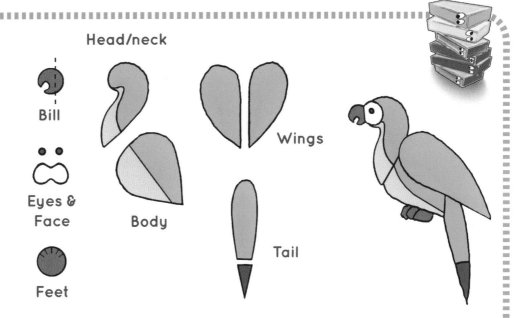

Head/neck

Bill

Eyes & Face

Body

Wings

Tail

Feet

The parrot is made from several tear-drop shapes and some altered balls of polymer. You can choose many bright colours.

To make the head and neck, make two identical avocado shaped tear-drops of yellow and green. These are cut so that a piece from each can be used to form the bird's head and neck ruff, with a yellow bib at the front. This two tone avocado shape is then bent and squeezed, as in the sequence below.

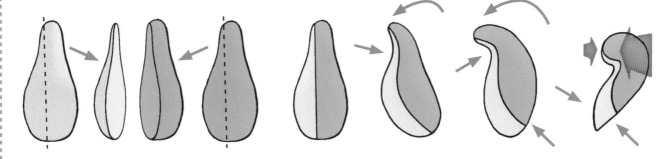

The same splicing technique is used for the body which is made of two fat tear-drops of yellow and green. The head / neck ruff can then be joined to the body.

The tail is made with a coloured tip spliced onto a long thin tear-drop shape. This is flattened before adding it to the body.

The wings are made of two flattened tear-drops of green polymer.

The white face of the parrot is a flattened oval of polymer which is pinched in the middle to make a shape that resembles a figure of eight lying on its side. This is folded onto the front of the head so that it makes the wide white patches around the eyes.

The parrots bill is a ball of orange which is flattened and given a notch with the point of a bamboo skewer. It is then shaped at the place where it joins the head with a vertical cut. This is then stuck onto the white polymer of the face.

The feet are made from a flattened ball of orange polymer which is given notches to suggest the bird's toes. This is where the skewer the bird stands on is inserted.

Pine Martens live in and around trees in remote parts of the Scottish Highlands and Islands. They have long bodies and tails and they are larger than stoats and weasels, at about 21 inches plus 10 inches for the tail.

While still being very rarely seen in the wild, they are making a comeback and extending their range southwards from the Highlands.

This clay project only models the front of the Pine Marten, as it is designed to be seen looking out from a plant pot.

Parts of the Pine Marten

The ears are made from a ball of clay which is dented with a paint brush handle and then cut into two parts

The head and body are made from one sausage of clay which is shaped and bent forward.

The eyes and nose are made from small balls of clay. Use a modelling tool or paint brush handle to make dents on the head where these features will go.

Use a modelling tool to shape the mouth just beneath the nose.

Once fired the model is painted with iron oxide. Iron oxide is rusted iron which will stick to ceramics when fired for a second time. If you are not firing your clay you can use brown paint - which will probably have iron oxide in it as a pigment.

Use a damp sponge to wipe off the oxide so that it reveals the texture and details of your model. If you like the eyes and nose can then be picked out with different colours.

The project needs to be fired again to permanently fix the iron oxide so that it will not rub or wash off.

You can make many other animals to look out of plant pots. If you are using air hardening clay you should varnish them so they do not take up water from the potting compost and go soggy.

This Pine Marten could be living in a flower pot near you!

Beads

Suitable for making with fired clay, air drying clay and polymer clay

Beads can be made very easily with balls of any sort of clay, just roll a ball in the palms of your hands and stick it on a bamboo skewer.

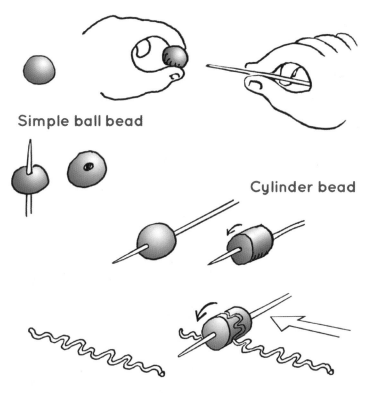

Simple ball bead

Cylinder bead

Rolling a cylinder bead over wiggly wire

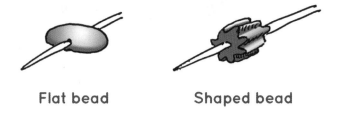

Flat bead   **Shaped bead**

String of beads

A ball shaped bead can be turned into a drum shaped bead by rolling it on the table with the skewer in the middle. Any bead can be given a pattern on the surface by rolling it over a texture. A wiggly line pattern can be made by bending a small piece of wire - like the wire used to close clay bags - and flattening it on the table to make an imprint in your beads.

Other bead shapes can be made by squashing or shaping with other tools. Keep the skewer in the bead until you have finished shaping it, then carefully pull it off and leave to dry.

If you are using **Fimo**® or any other polymer clay to make beads you will be able to do it in colour. Try blending different colours together for a marbled effect.

You can imitate this effect with coloured porcelain clay. Add coloured body stain powders to small amounts of porcelain and knead it to spread the colour evenly. Beads made from this material can look very attractive.

Multicoloured polymer bead

You can glaze biscuit fired clay beads and fire them again on special heat resistant wire. This is called **Ni-Chrome wire** and you will find it in an electric toaster used for the heating elements. You can also buy it from pottery suppliers. Make a clay support for your nichrome wire - called a **harp** - and string the glazed beads so that they are suspended above the kiln shelf. This is so they can be glazed all over without sticking to the kiln shelf.

A quarter of a teaspoon of high temperature stain is enough to colour a small lump of porcelain.

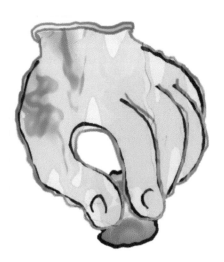

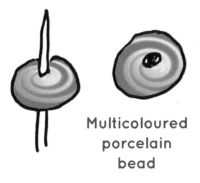

Multicoloured porcelain bead

Wear latex or rubber gloves to mix stains into clay by hand.

High temperature stain can be used to colour any clay but is particularly effective when mixed with white firing clay or porcelain. A marbled effect is possible when mixing differently coloured clays together.

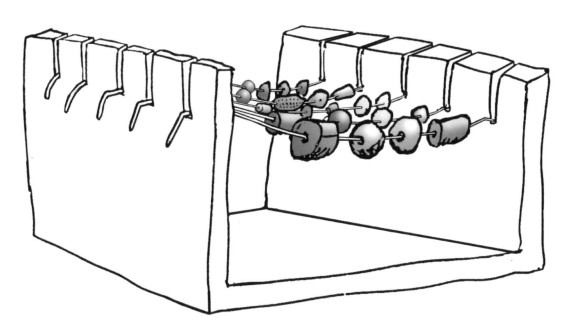

A fired clay harp with beads strung for glaze firing on Ni-Chrome wire

Blue cylinder beads made with grooves to take underglaze colour. The underglaze is painted on and then wiped away with a wet sponge. This leaves the colour in the grooves.

These beads have been fired without glaze to give a matt finish.

Glazed beads fired on Ni-Chrome rods, resting on kiln props. These ball shaped beads have been coated with black underglaze and then spattered with colour flicked from a tooth-brush. They were then painted with transparent glaze.

The red cylinder beads have been given wiggly grooves by rolling them on bent wire as they were made. They have transparent glaze which is wiped off the ends so they can be fired without the use of rods or wire, standing on end on the kiln shelf.

Clay beads threaded onto nylon cords

Polymer Clay beads made from a millefiori cane

Rub your beads with corn starch to remove finger prints from polymer clay before baking

A random selection of Polymer Clay beads

Threaded polymer clay beads

You can use up little bits of left over polymer clay from other projects by rolling them into beads. These can then be sorted and used for making bracelets, necklaces and cord pulls.

A Secret Island

This project uses natural clay for the ground and the lighter polymer clay for clouds.

The island is made from three clay thumb pots joined together to form a landscape. The larger one has had extra coils of clay added to it at the rim to make it taller, before turning it upside down. It has a rocky outcrop at the top which is made by hitting it with the corner of a stick.

The shallowest thumb pot is placed like an up-turned saucer at the base of the mountain.

All three thumb pots have been trimmed with a knife so they can fit neatly together.

Round holes of the same size have been cut so that the trees and building can be placed in different positions.

Small holes have been made in the mountain top so that Polymer Clay clouds can gather, supported on thin wires which represent rain falling.

The trees have been textured with the wiggly edge of a surform blade

Polymer Clay Clouds

Shaped coil for making the polymer clay clouds

The coil is rolled to make the stylised cloud

Holes are made with wire before the polymer cloud is baked

These pictures show the underglaze painting before the glaze has been added. The clouds and wires are taken off before glaze firing.

Fimo Effect® with glitter has been used to make the clouds

Inter-changeable pieces fit into all the different holes

The underglaze painting of the green parts has been put on in two layers. In the lower parts of the island blue is painted on first - it fades out as it gets higher up the slopes. Then green underglaze has been painted all over.

The brown parts in these pictures have been painted with iron oxide. The house and goat have been wiped with a sponge to bring out the details.

The transparent glaze is painted onto everything except the mountain top and the parts which fit closely together. This is because we don't want the glaze to block the tiny holes for the wires and the larger holes for the house and trees.

After glaze firing the blue under-painting is revealed. This is because the green underglaze becomes slightly transparent.

The iron oxide is fixed by the firing and will not rub off. The unglazed mountain top contrasts nicely with the glossy green areas.

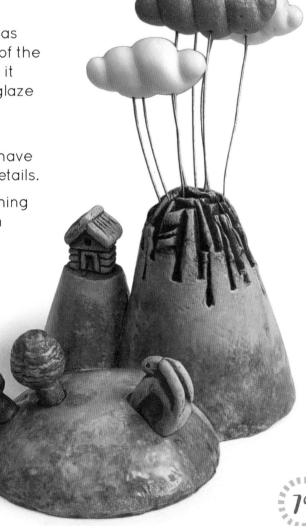

Pirate Gold

Made with fired clay or air drying clay and polymer clay

You can make your own tools for stamping patterns onto clay or polymer clay. If you have a kiln to biscuit fire your clay your stamps will last much longer. If you do not have a kiln then air hardening clay works best for stamps.

A fresh coin in mint condition

Stamps for minting your own polymer clay coins are made by rolling a small sausage of clay and cutting one end so that it finishes with a neat disc shaped surface. This is a blank for carving the image you want on your coins, it could be a symbol with your name, or the likeness of a pirate king, or any other suitable motif you can make small enough to go on a coin. It is good to make several designs on stamps so that you can choose the best ones to go into production with.

For best results leave the blank to harden off a bit to make it easier to carve. Then take a knife or modelling tools and make your mark. Remember that any dents into the blank will stick up on your finished coins.

When your stamp is finished leave it to dry out and fire it if you have a kiln. If you are using air drying clay to make your stamp, be sure to use well warmed up polymer for your coins.

Choose a suitable colour of polymer clay for the coins you are about to mint, then make several smooth round balls of it ready to try out your stamp. The rounder you make the ball the rounder your coin will be when it is squashed. Take your stamp and carefully squash the polymer clay ball leaving an imprint.

If you have made more than one stamp you can squash your coins between two stamps at once and get a two sided coin, heads and tails. Once stamped you may want to neaten up the edges of the coins. This can be done by trimming them with scissors or rolling them along their edges.

Clay stamps can be tested on soft clay when they are dry in order to fine tune finer detail. Any small thing that looks wrong can be corrected before biscuit firing. This is not necessary with air hardening clay as it can be carved after drying.

A selection of clay stamps and their imprints

Remember that writing has to be reversed on stamps, not just the letter order but the letter shapes too!

Heads

Pirates are very particular about spelling

Tails

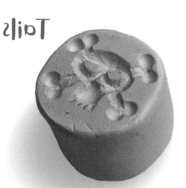

Heads

Tails

Mint your own coins

It is easier to judge how much polymer to use for each coin if you flatten a ball of polymer first to see how big a disc it will make. Then you can make a batch of balls of just the right size, ready to make your coins.

Balls of polymer clay ready to be stamped into coins

Biscuit fired clay stamps with Fimo® gold effect polymer clay

Balls pressed into flat discs

You can also use this technique to make badges and buttons.

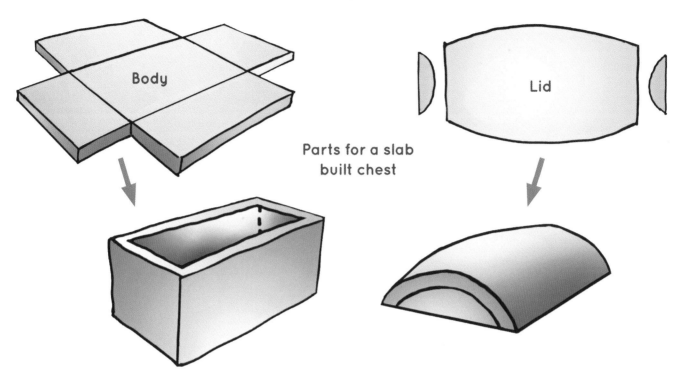

Parts for a slab built chest

To complete the treasure hoard you can build a clay chest to put the coins in. It should have a lid that fits and can be made to look like the sort of chest pirates might have used, with iron strapping and strong hinges. You can use slabs of clay to build the chest, or start with a chest shaped block of clay and hollow it out with a knife and a wire loop tool.

This treasure chest has been carved from a solid block of clay and then modelled to look as though it is built of wood and metal. The handles and other fittings were made separately and then stuck on.

Clay Play Gallery

Dog by Sofia

Whale by Sasha

Fox Tail by Finn

Steam Train by Orlagh

Cup by Nina

Crab by Ruby

Dog by Lucy

Meow-maid by Willow

Polymer Clay Play by Freya

Jellyfish by Freya

Garlic press action

Adding extruded strings

Sourcing Materials •••

It can be fun to look for clay deposits and dig some up to make things with. You may be lucky enough to have some under the soil in your garden. Sometimes you may find clay uncovered by rivers or the sea or by workers digging up the road. Always be careful when you find newly exposed clay deposits because the ground may still be unstable, particularly by the sea where rock falls can occur.

You can harden clay off a bit in an ordinary oven by turning it up as high as it will go and leaving your bone dried clay creations inside for a few hours. However, to make the irreversible transformation from clay to ceramic, you need a pottery kiln.

To get processed clays you can look for pottery suppliers online. In the U.K. you can buy clay from these suppliers, some of whom will sell small quantities for testing purposes.

- Valentines Clays Ltd. Valentine Way, Stoke-on-Trent ST4 2FJ
  www.valentineclays.co.uk
  T: +44 (0)1782 271200
  E: sales@ valentineclays.co.uk

- Bath Potters Supplies Ltd. Westfield Industrial Estate, Unit 18 Fourth Ave, Midsomer Norton, Radstock BA3 4XE
  www.bathpotters.co.uk
  T: +44 (0)1761 411077
  E: sales@ bathpotters.co.uk

- Potterycrafts Ltd. Campbell Road, Stoke-on-Trent ST4 4ET
  www.potterycrafts.co.uk
  T: +44 (0)1782 745000
  E: sales@ potterycrafts.co.uk

- Potclays Ltd. Brick Kiln Lane, Stoke-on-Trent ST4 7BP
  www.potclays.co.uk
  T: +44 (0)1782 219816
  E: sales@ potclays.co.uk

- Scarva Pottery Supplies, Unit 20 Scarva Rd Industrial Estate, Scarva Rd, Banbridge BT32 3QD
  www.scarva.com
  T: +44 (0)2840 669699
  E: sales@ scarva.com

To find Air Hardening Clay and Polymer Clay try your local art shop. If you can not find an art and craft supplier near where you live, search the internet.

Here are some reputable brands of Air Hardening Clay:

- DAS - An air-hardening modelling clay which is a versatile, fibrous, paper-based product. At first it is not very malleable, but with a little water and manipulation, the clay becomes more pliable. Because of the fibres in the clay, forms created with it are sturdy and less likely to break when dry than other products.

- Crayola Air-Dry Clay - This all-natural clay is safe for artists of all ages and dries within 24 hours to a hard, white surface good for painting or colouring with felt tipped pens. Note: because this clay shrinks when it dries, it works best for smaller projects; larger, thicker forms may develop cracks.

- STAEDTLER Fimo Air Basic Air Drying Modelling Clay - An air hardening clay from the makers of Fimo polymer clay.

- Scola nylon reinforced - Reinforced with synthetic fibres this clay is air drying with a low shrinkage rate. It can also be fired but needs ventilation to dispel the smoke from burning nylon fibre.
- Jovi Air-Dry - A very white modelling clay. Made in Barcelona, Spain, Jovi products are Non-toxic, CPSIA-certified, and gluten-free.

Here are some reputable brands of Polymer Clay:

- STAEDTLER Fimo Soft and Effect - Polymer clays from Germany which have a firm smooth texture and are relatively quick to condition. They can be used for all purposes including millefiori beads and sculpting. Durable after baking, they are firmer clays than Premo and Sculpey III but not as firm as Kato.
  Fimo Effect colours have special properties such as mica metallic, glitters, translucents, & faux stones. Fimo Soft has opaque colours.
- STAEDTLER Fimo Professional - Is a firm workable clay that does not get sticky and has a minimal smell. As it is based on high quality pigments Fimo Professional is perfect for colour mixing. The colour will not dull after baking and can be used in thin layers without tearing, which makes it perfect for making canes and sculpting. Firmer than Fimo Soft.
- Premo Sculpey - A polymer clay which has a ceramic like feel and allows for extremely detailed sculpting. It reaches a workable state with minimal conditioning and remains soft and pliable. A great clay for mixing colours and making millefiori canes, jewellery, and sculptures. Sculpey Premo is a strong and flexible Polymer clay and is not brittle after baking.
- Sculpey III - Is the softest brand of Polymer clay, it comes in many colours and be mixed with Fimo and Premo. When baked it has a matte finish but can be polished to a high shine if required. It is good for delicate or fine work but it is a little more brittle than the other brands
- Sculpey Soufflé - Is the latest clay released by Poly-form the makers of Sculpey and Premo clays. It is a lightweight clay perfect for jewellery making. Its strength and ability to hold detail makes it an excellent clay for making canes. It is strong and can also be used for larger projects, with a nice egg-shell finish when baked.
- Cernit - An opaque polymer clay in natural colours that resemble gemstones. This polymer clay bakes very hard.
- Kato - An artists quality Polymer clay from the USA developed by clay artist Donna Kato. This clay is excellent to work with, but is harder to condition than Premo or Sculpey. It is a firm and non sticky clay after working which is an advantage in warmer climates, and when baked is strong and flexible. Excellent for beads, caning and fine detail work. This clay bakes at a higher temperature to the other brands so this has to be taken into account when mixing with them.

Glossary

Ashes: The greyish powder and unburned bits that are sometimes left inside hollow projects that were made with newspaper for support.

Batt: A 1/4 inch to 3/4 inch thick flat, wooden, or plastic disc that fits over the wheel-head of a potter's wheel. It is used to throw a pot on the wheel or to dry a pot when the bat is removed from the wheel. Sometimes it's square.

Batt pegs: The pegs on the wheel-head of a potter's wheel that hold the batt in place.

Biscuit or bisque-ware: Any unglazed or under-glazed ceramic piece that has been fired at a low temperature before glazing. Bisque-ware usually means something that has been biscuit fired in the kiln.

Biscuit firing: The first firing in the kiln at a low temperature (usually cone 010 to 04). This is how bisque-ware is made.

Body (clay body): Any blend of clays and non-plastic ceramic materials that you can work with. Clay bodies are designed to become hard and ceramic at certain firing temperatures.

Bone-dry: A drying stage when your project is completely air dried and all the moisture is gone. Both white and red clay will become lighter and look "chalky".

Brushing: Applying slip or glaze using a paint brush.

Burnishing: The process of polishing clay with a polished stone or spoon and some vegetable oil to give the surface of a pot a high-gloss finish without using glazes.

Centring: A wheel-throwing skill which involves the shaping of a ball of clay into an even form in the centre of the spinning potter's wheel.

Centrifugal force: A force that tends to make spinning bodies (like clay walls) move away from the centre.

Ceramics: Objects made from earthy materials that are transformed through a heat process. Also the process of making these objects.

Clay: A variety of earthy materials formed by the breakdown of granite rocks over millions of years. Can be combined with other materials to form different types of clay bodies.

Clay body: See Body.

Clear glaze: A clear coating that melts onto the clay surface with the use of heat. It will form a dull or glossy finish when fired to a certain temperature.

Coil: A long roll of clay that has been formed by hand. It can look like a snake or a worm.

Coiling: A handbuilding method that uses many coils to build walls, handles, etc. The coils are smoothed together to form a sturdy structure.

Collaring: A wheel-throwing method that prevents clay walls from expanding out (caused by centrifugal force). It is the act of pushing your cylinder walls gently toward the centre.

Conditioning: Of polymer clay. The word conditioning is used to describe the process of warming up polymer clay by kneading it.

Cone: A small cone-shaped piece of ceramic material that is sensitive to heat. It is placed inside the kiln to reveal the amount of heat work being done. When the measuring cone bends you know the glaze will be fully melted. This is more useful than only measuring temperature in the kiln.

Crank Clay: Clay that is coarse in texture and suitable for making larger sculptures. Crank Clay has a higher proportion of coarse grog to clay than finer clays which are more suitable for throwing.

Cut-off tool or Cheese Wire: A tool used to cut off chunks of clay. It is a long piece of wire string attached to wooden handles at both ends.

Cylinder: A cylinder is a tube shape that is first formed on the potter's wheel after centring.

Decorative use only: A warning that a project should not be used for food or for holding liquid. It's only for looking at. These projects do not have a protective coating, so ceramic dust may get on food, and water will likely leak.

Dipping: A method of applying glaze to a project by dunking it in a bucket of glaze.

Drying: The natural removal of moisture from a project by the air. If you don't dry your project long enough before firing, it may crack or explode in the kiln.

Firing: The process of heating pottery and sculptures in a kiln or open fire.

Fettling knife: A carving knife with a narrow, round tip. It is used for cutting into leather-hard clay.

Foot: The base of a pot. The part that it stands on.

Foot pedal: The pedal on an electric potter's wheel that controls the speed of the spinning wheel.

Glaze: Any glass-like coating that melts onto the clay surface with the use of heat. It will form a dull or glossy finish when fired to the required heat level.

Glaze firing: The second firing that heats and melts the glaze to form a glassy coating on the surface.

Green-ware: Any unfired project that is leather-hard or bone-dry.

Handbuilding: A general term that means the process of making pottery and ceramic sculptures by hand, rather than on a potter's wheel. It usually refers to pinch, coil, and slab building methods.

Kick-wheel: A potter's wheel that is powered by kicking a rotating wheel with your foot.

Kiln: A special furnace or clay oven designed to safely increase heat to 1300° C, or cone 10.

Leather-hard: A drying stage that occurs after your project has been air-dried about one day indoors, or as fast as 20 minutes in direct sunlight. The clay stiffens and holds its shape, but can still be easily carved.

Low-fire: Firing that does not exceed 1070°C, or Cone 04.

Low-fire clay: Clay that is designed to become hard and ceramic at low-fire temperatures in the kiln.

Millefiori Canes: Polymer clay can be made into sticks or "canes" with a coloured pattern running through them. These canes can be stretched thin to make very detailed small patterns which are sliced up and made into intricate designs.

Mould: Any hard form that can be used to shape a ceramic project.

Mosaic: A picture or design made from small bits of ceramics, small stones, or pieces of polymer clay.

Neck: The narrow area of a pot below a flared opening.

Nichrome wire: A heat-resistant wire that will not melt in the kiln during firing. It is made from an alloy of Nickel and Chrome.

Oxides: A loose term used by potters to describe all metal colouring oxides and carbonates, such as iron oxide, cobalt oxide or carbonate, copper oxide or carbonate, and many others.

Pinch or pinching: The handbuilding method of squeezing clay between your thumb and fingers to form a pot or sculpture.

Plasticity: The quality of clay that enables it to bend and stretch without cracking.

Polymer: Polymers are materials made of long, repeating chains of molecules. The term polymer is often used to describe plastics, which are synthetic polymers.

Porcelain: A fine white translucent clay body that is more difficult to work with than low-fire clays. It behaves a bit like polymer clay in that it has lower plasticity.

Pot: In ceramics, any vessel or object made of clay.

Potter's wheel: A revolving wheel that is used to create pottery. It can be powered by foot or by electricity.

Pottery: Any ceramic object as well as the workshop where it is made.

Scoring: A method for attaching two pieces of clay by scratching the areas where they attach, applying slip, then smoothing and sealing the edges.

Sgraffito: An under-glazing decorating method of scraping away a design into the underglaze on a project. This allows the clay body to show through. Ideal for use on leather-hard projects.

Shrinkage: This is a process which clay goes through, getting slightly smaller as it dries. As moisture leaves the clay it shrinks.

Slab building: A handbuilding method that uses flat, even pieces of clay about 1/2 inch thick that are formed with a rolling pin.

Slip: A mixture of clay and water. It is used like glue, as part of the joining process with scoring. Coloured slip can also be used for decorating.

Smoke firing: A decorative firing method that is used on bisque-fired projects. Flammable materials like newspaper, straw, or pine needles are put in a metal rubbish bin with the project, then set on fire so the smoke can darken the surface of the pots.

Splash pan: The part of the potter's wheel where extra water and slushy clay is captured.

Surform Tool: A tool used for removing clay by scraping. The surform blade resembles a small cheese grater. It works best on leather hard clay.

Trimming: The removal of extra clay from the foot or the body of wheel-thrown projects to refine the shape. This is done on the potter's wheel with a trimming tool.

Underglaze: Any colouring material used under a glaze. This is applied to green-ware and then bisque-fired

Underglaze pencils: Under-glazes available in pencils, so detailed designs can be drawn directly on the project.

Wedging: The process of removing trapped air inside the clay by kneading the clay. This is especially important when combining pieces of clay, recycling clay, or preparing clay for use on the potter's wheel.

Wheel-head: The part of the potter's wheel that rotates and spins.

Index

Thank you for reading.

If you enjoyed this book, please consider leaving an honest review at your favourite shop, on social media or on your blog.

#ClayPlayBook